# New York

D0453665

A guide to recent architecture

•••

Susanna Sirefman
Photographs by Keith Collie

# New York

A guide to recent architecture

● ● ● ellipsis KÖNEMANN

•••

All rights reserved. No part of this publication may be reproduced in any form without written permission from the publisher

CREATED, EDITED AND DESIGNED BY
Ellipsis London Limited
55 Charlotte Road London EC2A 3QT
E MAIL ...@ellipsis.co.uk
WWW http://www.ellipsis.co.uk/ellipsis
PUBLISHED IN THE UK AND AFRICA BY
Ellipsis London Limited
SERIES EDITOR Tom Neville
EDITOR Vicky Wilson
SERIES DESIGN Jonathan Moberly
LAYOUT Pauline Harrison
PHOTOGRAPH OF SUSANNA SIREFMAN
reproduced by kind permission of Wah

COPYRIGHT © 1997 Könemann
Verlagsgesellschaft mbH
Bonner Straße 126, D-50968 Köln
PRODUCTION MANAGER Detlev Schaper
PRINTING AND BINDING Sing Cheong
Printing Ltd
Printed in Hong Kong

ISBN 3 89508 641 X (Könemann)
ISBN 1 899858 32 6 (Ellipsis)

**Susanna Sirefman 1997**

# Contents

**Introduction**

This guide is not intended as a comprehensive directory of recent buildings but as an urbanistic overview of New York City's architectural topography and its alteration over the last decade – an urban study rather than an arbitrary look at individual projects.

Nicknamed Gotham City, Metropolis, the Big Apple, New York City is perhaps the sexiest city in the world. Definitely delirious, ambitiously hyperactive, tranquil and elegant, Manhattan, in particular, is the quintessence of gritty urban glamour. An overcrowded island with skyscrapers crammed together, the insertion of any new building creates a domino effect. One edifice can send ripples of change throughout the vicinity. This dynamic energy (despite shockingly conservative architecture) combined with a vast vertical scale is part of what gives New York its pizzazz.

Most built work of the last decade heavily involves the infrastructure of the city. New architecture defines pockets of change, chunks of development – Bryant Park, Central Park, South Street Seaport, Lower Manhattan, Battery Park City, Union Square, Clinton, Madison Avenue and the 42nd Street Development Plan to name a few. The outer boroughs – Brooklyn, Bronx and Queens – also have neighbourhoods undergoing regeneration, some more successfully than others. The 663-foot-tall Skidmore, Owings & Merrill Citicorp skyscraper in Queens thankfully failed to attract other corporate towers, but downtown Brooklyn – already a bustling, relatively erect civic centre – has seen a number of recent large building additions.

I have blurred both the temporal and programmatic boundaries of the last decade. My ten-year timeline has been stretched at both ends to include Der Scutt's Trump Tower (dating back to 1983) – an indisputable icon of the booming 1980s – as well as a 'future' entry describing the ongoing saga of Times Square. A plethora of new building did not occur in the early 1990s – skyscrapers are just starting to rise again. For this reason I have also included a few intriguing reuse and rehab projects. Many of these are at a civic scale: the long-dormant Ellis Island immigration station has been magically transformed into a celebratory Museum of Immigration; the original site for a major department store in Murray Hill – B Altman's – is now New York's Business and Science Library; an old landmarked warehouse in Queens has metamorphosed into the additively volumetric container for the American Museum of the Moving Image. A subject of much discussion within the architectural community, many architects hope this turn-around phase will be a catalyst for future new buildings.

Much of the city's electric charge derives from its diverse population of 7 million inhabitants. The emphasis in the last few years on redesigned public space – streets, squares, plazas – is evidence that New Yorkers really use their public realm. This is amusingly apparent in midtown Manhattan during weekday lunchhours when the streets suddenly become alive with fast-food vendors and in warm weather people sit on steps, barriers and benches. Times Square at any hour affords a Technicolor view of this mad rush of swarming activity. Cesar Pelli's World Financial Center in Battery Park City embraces its spectacular site with a 3.5-acre waterside esplanade that is heavily used in all seasons – an exemplary architectural attempt to be socially responsible. The contrast with the adjacent, brutally isolationist World Trade Center (Minoru Yamasaki, 1976) has forced the Port Authority (owners of the Trade Towers) to rethink their dreadful, forever-empty plaza.

The infinite programmatic possibility for so many species of public is daunting. This is a city where *savoir faire* lives side by side with boorishness. One cannot simply buy a lettuce at the corner shop – it must be

**New York: a guide to recent architecture**

either arugula, romaine, endive or, when slumming it, field greens – yet one can purchase a cheap $5 fortune from a doubtful-looking fortune teller on many street corners. In the poshest of neighbourhoods, cigar power clubs sit behind $1 hotdog stands. Cliques of *très* unchic cigarette smokers are becoming the new street furniture outside their towering office blocks, constantly passed by never-ending troops of Prada-clad tourists.

All this adds up to a delicious *savoir vivre*.

Although every New Yorker is busy 'being somebody' and so are its buildings in one fashion or another, this has not prevented an epidemic of regrettable architectural conservatism. Many structures designed in the 1980s simply shout glossy corporate image: Philip Johnson's AT&T Building, Skidmore, Owings & Merrill's Worldwide Plaza, Edward Larrabee Barnes Associates' Equitable Center, Murphy/Jahn's CitySpire and 750 Lexington Avenue. Madison Avenue's posh 'strip mall' has been transformed into the ultimate global advertising street with hugely expensive high-end retail designer showcases vying vehemently to outglam one another. These pretentiously over-the-top venues range in style from Ralph Lauren's more-British-than-the-British grand Rhinelander Mansion on Madison Avenue and East 72nd Street to John Pawson's first New York minimalist white box, for Calvin Klein. This extraordinary retail trend has spilled out on to the nearby 57th Street strip, where newcomers such as Chanel, Niketown and Warner Brothers have attracted a diversity of customers who have contributed to the considerable suburbanisation of Manhattan. Thankfully these projects are not inward-turning vertical malls (like the Trump Tower) and though most are grandiose efforts at bad architecture, each shop does make an effort to maintain the city's street wall.

New York: a guide to recent architecture

Capitalism at its greediest has had a stultifying effect on the New York City skyline, quashing the possibility of the new, the avant-garde. It is shocking how parochial and strait-laced contemporary architecture in Manhattan can be. Though New York is at the cutting edge in progressive art, this is sadly not the case for architecture. The explanation must be economics. Manhattan is about making money, the perpetual race for the greenback. Skyscrapers and designer showcases are no more than mercantile products, a business device. The developer's – and therefore the architect's – primary concern is marketability, saleability and rentability.

Peculiar measures are taken to save money. A fascinating example is the office tower at 320 Park Avenue, reconstructed by Swanke Hayden Connell (architects of the Trump Tower) in 1995. Originally built a few months before a change in zoning laws, this 34-storey skyscraper has one and a half times as much floor space as a new building on the same site would be allowed to contain. So the structural core of the building was retained and $73 million spent on reconstruction. Minor alterations were made to floor space and the mechanical core was expanded. The big change was the recladding of the exterior and the apex's metamorphosis from a flat top to a gabled peak.

Zoning laws dictate much of Manhattan's structural form. Setbacks, trade-offs and requirements for public space are extremely detailed. The city government takes zoning issues very seriously. An almost completed condominium apartment building at 108 East 96th Street had to remove 12 floors in the mid 1980s as it was found to be in violation of local height restrictions. An allegedly complicated case, this raised much discussion of New York's ever-changing zoning regulations.

Battery Park City and Times Square are both instances of heavily

**New York: a guide to recent architecture**

mandated zoning laws working against the possibility of urban spontaneity. Battery Park City has extremely strict guidelines (masterplan by Cooper, Eckstut Associates) that follow a neo-traditional style. As a result, the project resembles a planned community despite the large number of architectural firms involved.

In 1993 Robert A M Stern and graphic designer Tibor Kalman of the firm M&Co devised standards for the size, scale and placement of signage on West 42nd Street's street wall. Heavily criticised as 'urban taxidermy', their sentimental directives have created a sensaround, jumbotron enclave that suggests virtual reality. A simulation of a simulation, this is a nostalgic version of the past that is bigger and better than what actually existed. But this does not mean to say that West 42nd Street is not still powerful. It gets me every time I approach that bowtie junction – that soppy 'I Love New York' feeling comes on instantly, proving that visual planning, like lush movie music, can create the desired effect.

In addition to the New York architectural scene still being very much a man's world, rampant conservatism also means that many internationally celebrated architects who maintain offices in Manhattan do not build here. Richard Meier has constructed nothing in New York City in 20 years. Michael Graves designed a shopfront in Manhattan well over ten years ago and Aldo Rossi, who has a Manhattan office, has never built here. Steven Holl, Gaetano Pesce and Arata Isozaki have all done amazing interior work but next to no complete buildings (Holl does have a delectable tiny project downtown, the Storefront for Art & Architecture). It would be a delight to see these architects do large-scale work in the city.

The outer boroughs are more architecturally adventurous. I have happily included Rafael Viñoly's buildings in the Bronx and Queens, Peter Eisenman's only New York project – a fire station in Brooklyn – and

Robert A M Stern's two buildings in Brooklyn. These are all interesting intellectual architectural pleasures and it is Manhattan's loss that more advantage is not taken of such amazing local talent.

Despite these gripes, there is still no city quite like New York. Lovable, romantic and thrilling, the tangible energy of the grid, the mountainous skyscape and the swarms of diverse inhabitants have created the most extraordinary place.

ACKNOWLEDGEMENTS
I thank you: to all the architects I met with who were so generous with their time and materials; to Keith Collie for his superb photography; to Tom Neville for his quiet encouragement; to Barbara Orlando and Margaret Kaminski of MTA New York City Transit for their advice on public transport; to Frederic Schwartz for his wisdom; to Kar-Hwa Ho for his knowledge; but most of all an enormous thank you to four true-blue New Yorkers – Carol and Josef Sirefman, Joshua Sirefman and Alexander Shapiro – whose passionate enthusiasm for their native city was a constant source of inspiration.
SS 1997

**New York: a guide to recent architecture**

# How to use this book

New York City is an aggregation of five diverse boroughs. This guide includes four of them: Manhattan, Brooklyn, Queens and the Bronx. The guide is divided geographically: Manhattan has 11 sections beginning with Lower Manhattan and moving north through Morningside Heights and Harlem. The outer boroughs follow as separate sections.

New York is a splendid city for walking. A doddle to navigate, Manhattan's street pattern is a grid starting above 14th Street. The avenues run north–south and the numbered streets east–west. Broadway is the landmark exception to the grid – originally an Algonquin Indian trade route trail it runs north–south in a diagonal, swerving from the west to the east side at its lower termination. Manhattan started at the southern tip of the island and the already well-established streets below 14th Street escaped the 1811 imposition of the Cartesian grid.

The nearest subway station and bus route for each entry is listed. An important part of New York's infrastructure, public transport, although gritty, is reliable and convenient. As in any major city, do be streetwise.

MTA New York City Transit's Travel Information Center is reachable at 718 330 1234, 24 hours daily. The New York Convention and Visitors Bureau Information Center gives travel directions over the phone at 212 397 8222 between 9.00 and 18.00 weekdays and 10.00 and 18.00 at weekends.

When visiting the boroughs be sure to take advantage of the fact that Manhattan is an island. Excellent spots to look upon this jam-packed vertical extravaganza are Columbia Heights in Brooklyn, Promenade in Brooklyn, Roosevelt Tramway (Second Avenue at West 59th Street), Hoboken Ferry, Ellis Island Ferry and the Triborough Bridge. These magical cinematic perspectives exemplify the fact that Manhattan from a distance, as well as up close, always delivers a euphoric punch.

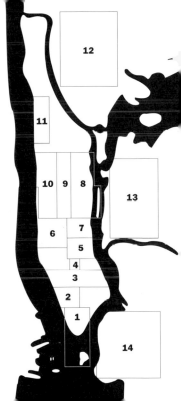

# Lower Manhattan

# Ellis Island Museum of Immigration

At the turn of the 20th century this was the immigrant's gateway to America. Ellis Island's visual proximity to Manhattan and prime view of the Statue of Liberty made arrival here a formidably symbolic experience. Even today, looking back at the vertical Legoland of the city, one can imagine how a hopeful immigrant might have felt. Yet Ellis Island was not always about the American dream.

Known as Gull Island, it was originally a 3-acre sandbar owned by the Mohegan Indians. Occupied by Dutch settlers in 1661, it was renamed Oyster Island. Going through more reincarnations than a poorly chosen restaurant venue, it was a convenient locale for hanging pirates in the mid 18th century. Samuel Ellis purchased it in 1780 and ran a tavern there before selling it to the federal government in the early 1800s.

Until the last decade of the 19th century, would-be immigrants simply had to arrive in America. Informal processing was done at the nearby Castle Clinton, but there were no federal laws about who could or couldn't settle. With the creation of the Federal Bureau of Immigration in 1891, Ellis Island became America's immigrant filtering station. As Fort Gibson, Ellis was increased to 14 acres and then to 27.5 acres using earth excavated during the construction of the New York City subway system. Island-ownership battles continue: recently the state of New Jersey filed a lawsuit against the state of New York claiming its right to 24 acres of landfill, though New Jersey does not dispute New York's ownership of the original 3-acre rock.

After the immigration station ceased to function in 1932, Ellis became a detention centre for 'enemies of the United States', accommodating German nationals and other alleged enemies during the two world wars and suspected subversives following the Internal Security Act of 1950. The island was abandoned in 1954.

**Lower Manhattan**

**Beyer Blinder Belle 1990**

**Beyer Blinder Belle 1990**

The immigration station buildings (35 in all) were designed to overawe new arrivals. The entry pavilion has a triple-height archway leading to the main registry room – 200 feet long, 100 feet wide with a 56-foot vaulted ceiling. The brick façade, in French Renaissance style, was fronted by a long glass and cast-iron canopy. Now the main entrance to the museum, the renovated space is still awe-inspiring.

Renovation took eight years. The main building was in such poor condition it took two years to dry out. Two large heaters outside the structure combined with pressurised dry air inside got rid of the excess moisture. Weatherproofing was then done and repairs made to damaged windows, walls and floors.

The big architectural questions Beyer Blinder Belle needed to resolve were: which time period to depict, what to conserve, and what to replicate? The era between 1918 and 1924 was chosen because this was the peak period of use as an immigration station. Three new architectural gestures form the organisational basis for the design: the registry staircase, known as the 'staircase of sighs' was recreated; a new 114-foot canopy was placed in the footprint of the old one; and a terrace off the original confectionary (now a cafeteria) was added.

ADDRESS Ellis Island, New York Harbor
CLIENT Statue of Liberty/Ellis Island Foundation/US Department of the Interior, National Park Service
STRUCTURAL ENGINEER Robert Silman Associates
COST $156 million
SIZE 220,415 square feet (20,477 square metres)
SUBWAY 1/9 to South Ferry; 4, 5 to Bowling Green BUS M1, M6, M15
ACCESS open

**Lower Manhattan**

**Beyer Blinder Belle 1990**

Lower Manhattan

**Seamen's Church Institute**

An AIA Awards Jury tagged this building 'a textbook example of contextualism'. Certainly its nautical theme is widely evident in its site: South Street Seaport, an 11-block historic district posing as a theme park, its stone-paved streets of 18th- and 19th-century fishmongers' and ships-traders' quarters now converted into shops, restaurants and museums.

The Seamen's Church Institute is a 155-year-old organisation that looks after merchant seafarers. Contained within its headquarters are an ecumenical chapel, the Seafarers Club, legal offices, a gallery, a training institute and two ground-floor retail spaces.

An integral part of the design process was the need to incorporate a four-storey building already on the site – a Dutch colonial ship chandlery dating from 1799. The early and recent façades are artfully knit together by an existing quoined service entrance. The old edifice's proportions and materials – brick, granite and steel – are replicated in the new.

Clad in white porcelain-enamelled steel, the exterior is surprisingly fun. Ostensibly influenced by Corb, Aalto and Pierre Chareau, this is a literal interpretation of a shiplike edifice. All control over the marine theme was lost on the upper two storeys. A beacon to seafarers on the roof emphasises the likeness to the upper decks of a ship and even the airy interiors replicate decks organised around a central circular stack. A yardarm flying the institute's colours surmounts the entire composition.

ADDRESS 241 Water Street
STRUCTURAL ENGINEER Robert Silman Associates
COST $8 million SIZE 32,000 square feet (2970 square metres)
SUBWAY 2, 3, 4, 5, J, M to Fulton Street; A, C to Broadway/Nassau Street BUS M15, M22
ACCESS ground floor, museum and chapel open

**James Stewart Polshek and Partners Architects 1991**

Lower Manhattan

**James Stewart Polshek and Partners Architects 1991**

# TBWA Chiat/Day

The creation of a new architectural typology is not a common interest or a practical possibility for most contemporary practitioners. Venetian architect Gaetano Pesce is the exception. Obsessed with new materials, future technologies and revolutionary ways to inhabit space, Pesce has invented a new version of the office. Whether the design and programme succeed in stirring up creative juices – as is the intention – remains to be seen, but this certainly is a sunny, funny, squishy place.

Jay Chiat collaborated closely with Pesce to create this forward-looking 'virtual office'. Chiat commissioned Lubowicki/Lanier Architects to design an LA interior (in a previously commissioned Frank Gehry building) at the same time.

The programme required an audio-visual production centre, video room, art studio, conference rooms, social area, individual lockers and a lounge/cafeteria. The architectural superstructure called for deterritorialisation: a fluid, non-hierarchical formation of space. The result is an enchanting playground on the 37th and 38th floors of a typical Lower Manhattan office tower. Employees arrive as and when they desire, laptops and cellular phones are checked out from an electronic dispensary disguised as a pair of huge, Chanel-red lips, and personal lockers resembling human profiles afford the only privacy.

The overall plan is based on an Italian village. There is a Piazza, Clubhouse, Doghouse and a rolling staircase meant as a roving public platform with all political connotations intended. The site is endowed with a spectacular panoramic view of Manhattan and its waterfront. Pesce's clever layout creates narrow streets and alleys that explode into perspectival views. Wall surfaces are quick witted and unexpected – TV remote controls and video cassettes are laid like bricks; elsewhere walls are lined like padded cells. Polyester, resin, rubber and felt abound.

**Lower Manhattan**

**Gaetano Pesce 1994**

Pesce forsees society as moving towards communication through imagery. His amusing iconography includes doorways in the shape of client products and seductive images drawn on the blood-orange and aquamarine resin floor. To create this most refined and beautiful floor finish, pigmented resin was poured at a 7-millimetre thickness on to a smooth concrete slab and drawings were cast by hand within the half hour the resin took to set.

**Lower Manhattan**

ADDRESS 38th floor, 180 Maiden Lane
STRUCTURAL ENGINEER Thornton Thomasetti
SIZE 50,000 square feet (4600 square metres)
SUBWAY 2, 3, 4, 5, J, Z to Fulton Street; A, C to Broadway/Nassau Street
BUS M1, M6
ACCESS none; agency may request visitors' fee!

**Gaetano Pesce 1994**

Lower Manhattan

**Gaetano Pesce 1994**

# Battery Park City

Battery Park City, a title suggestive of a city within the city, is a misnomer. The development seems more of a suburban appendage on the south-western edge of Manhattan, isolated physically from the rest of the city by the eight-lane highway of West Street. Driven by an unusual combination of public and private interests, the hugely ambitious, $4 billion undertaking has received mixed criticism.

The project is built on 92 acres of landfill culled from excavations made during the construction of the 110-storey World Trade Center. The masterplan, drawn up over a period of 90 days, focused on the public realm, prioritising the allocation of open spaces. The 1.2-mile Esplanade runs the entire length of the waterfront, with the result that a quarter of the site functions as a public park. Manhattan's Cartesian street grid then continues on to the rest of the new land designated as a commercial area surrounded by two residential neighbourhoods (14,000 apartments in total) known as Rector Place and Battery Place. Cooper, Eckstut hoped that by allocating small parcels to different developer–architect teams, an intrinsically urban diversity would emerge.

But the guidelines were too strict, insisting on a neo-traditional style based on conventional notions of the street and square, with the result that despite the large number of architectural firms involved, the project still resembles a planned community. Lower Manhattan is a higgledy-piggledy arrangement of winding streets; the meticulous organisation of Battery Park City works against spontaneity, a primary feature of cities. Social stratification adds to the homogeneity: rentals and condominiums are all high end, appealing to the bankers who work in the nearby financial centre. (The state government has introduced a slightly bizarre scheme whereby a percentage of Battery Park City's revenue is allocated to low-income housing in other areas of Manhattan.) And the relentless

**Cooper, Eckstut Associates 1979–97**

Lower Manhattan

**Cooper, Eckstut Associates 1979–97**

tidiness achieved by the private security and cleaning force only serves to exacerbate the sterile quality of the development.

On a more positive note, the river frontage is marvellous, as are the commercial buildings, developed by Olympia & York and designed by Cesar Pelli (see World Financial Center, page 28). A contiguous chain of parks runs the entire length of the Hudson with the ritzy North Cove yacht harbour as the centrepoint. Each park has its own flavour as several artists were invited to create interventions. South Cove is a rambling, rocky park with a timber spiralling stair designed by artist Mary Miss in collaboration with landscape architect Susan Child and architect Stanton Eckstut. The most recently completed park is the F Wagner Jr Park designed by architects Machado & Silvetti in collaboration with landscape architects Olin Partnership. Among the other artists involved are Ned Smythe, Richard Artschwager and Martin Puryear.

ADDRESS bound by Battery Park to the south, Chambers Street to the north, West Street to the east and the Hudson River to the west MASTERPLAN AND DESIGN GUIDELINES Cooper, Eckstut Associates PARTICIPATING ARCHITECTS Cesar Pelli & Associates; Adamson Associates; Haines Lundberg Waehler; Charles Moore with Rothzeid Kaiserman Thomson & Bee; Davis, Brody & Associates; James Stewart Polshek and Partners Architects; Conklin Rossant; Mitchell/Giurgola; Gruzen Samton Steinglass; Bond Ryder James; Ulrich Franzen/The Vilkas Group; Alexander Cooper & Associates; Ehrenkrantz, Eckstut & Whitelaw; Costas Kondylis
COST $4 billion
SUBWAY 1/9 to Rector Street; N, R to Cortlandt Street
BUS M9, M10
ACCESS parks, lobbies and facilities open

**Lower Manhattan**

**Cooper, Eckstut Associates 1979–97**

**Cooper, Eckstut Associates 1979–97**

# World Financial Center

The World Financial Center, nearly 7 million square feet of office space, is Battery Park City's commercial component. The complex is composed of four office towers, a glass-roofed courtyard (Winter Garden), two gateway buildings and a 3.5-acre landscaped public plaza.

Cesar Pelli: 'The city is more important than the building; the building is more important than the architect. I connect with what is strongest in each place, drawing on its positive qualities and compensating for the negative.' Pelli's good intentions are clear in this vast project. The entire complex addresses the street wall beautifully, striving to deal with the peculiarities and delights of the site and to engage with the world at a human scale. Beautiful and important as icons, the monolithic twin towers of Minoru Yamasaki's adjacent World Trade Center (completed in 1976) seem isolated from present public realities. There are now plans to develop the vast, empty plaza between the 110-storey slab, inspired by the urbanistic and financial success of the World Financial Center.

The public focus of Pelli's project is the Winter Garden. The glass barrel-vaulted roof is 125 feet high, 120 feet wide and 200 feet long. An outer perimeter of eateries and retail outlets loops around this 18,000-square-foot meeting place, which is used by as many as 35,000 people an hour. A grand marble staircase creates an amphitheatre facing a grove of 16 90-foot palm trees. This pleasingly camp space with its extravagant marble floor is the perfect setting for an elaborate series of free cultural events, and people in diverse attire rest on the marble steps day and night. Likened to Joseph Paxton's Crystal Palace, constructed for Britain's Great Exhibition of 1851, the space is subtly tranquillising through its sheer vastness and fantastic view of the Hudson River.

The Winter Garden extends outside into elegantly designed parkland – an outdoor plaza that rejoices in its waterfront location. The fabulous

**Cesar Pelli & Associates 1988**

**Cesar Pelli & Associates 1988**

granite street furniture echoes the forms of the surrounding buildings. Paradise for rollerbladers, cyclists and joggers, this is a wonderfully calm part of the city. The Statue of Liberty, Ellis Island and the Verrazano Bridge create a backdrop for the splendid helicopter-capped yachts parked in the exclusive North Cove Marina.

The four stocky towers (ranging from 34 to 51 storeys) are topped by distinctive shapes: a mastaba, a dome, a stepped pyramid and a pure pyramid. The massing was requested by the developers, who foresaw the need for larger floor areas. Borderline po-mo, the toy-block imagery is redeemed by the dazzling surface texture. As each glass and granite building grows upwards out of its granite-sheathed base, the relationship between window and granite changes until finally the towers are clad solely in glass skins. The copper hats on the top ground the tapering effect of the reflective glass.

ADDRESS Battery Park City, bordered by the Hudson River, West Street, Vesey Street and Liberty Street
CLIENT Olympia & York Equity Corporation
ASSOCIATE ARCHITECTS Adamson Associates (Toronto); Haines Lundberg Waehler (New York)
STRUCTURAL ENGINEER Lev Zetlin Associates, M S Yolles & Partners
SIZE 8.9 million square feet (827,000 square metres)
SUBWAY 1, 2, 3, 9, N, R to Cortlandt Street; C, E to World Trade Center
BUS M9, M10, M22
ACCESS lobbies and Winter Garden open

**Cesar Pelli & Associates 1988**

Lower Manhattan

**Cesar Pelli & Associates 1988**

# Stuyvesant High School

This strange, monolithic building seems more appropriate to a high-powered financial centre than to an educational institution for talented teenagers. The most expensive public high school to be built in America and the first in New York City for over a decade, Stuyvesant has its own satellite, computer system and a $500,000 photography laboratory. A marble and granite corporate fantasy, it is the only high school I can recall visiting that has a reception desk. With its ten escalators, 65 classrooms, 650-seat cafeteria, 850-seat auditorium and swimming pool with touch pads and timers, it resembles an expensive private college. Corporate-style materials and a business-like atmosphere permeate the unfortunate structure.

The nation's best academic high school, Stuyvesant is one of three New York institutions specialising in maths and science. Famous for its illustrious alumni, including my father and several Nobel prize-winners, the school was established 90 years ago. Nearly 3000 students are selected through a competitive examination.

Following its move from a deteriorating 1907 Beaux-Arts building, Stuyvesant was leased the new site by New York State for an annual fee of $1. The spectacular, triangular urban-edge plot at the northernmost tip of Battery Park City is bordered by three different city conditions: the axial street grid of Battery Park City to the south; the Hudson River to the north; and the Route 9A highway to the east. The panoramic view of the Statue of Liberty, the World Trade Center and the World Financial Center creates the sense of being at the centre of the world.

The three different aspects of the city that form its borders informed the school's final design. The south façade is symmetrical and dressy; facing the waterfront are three smaller-scale parts; the east elevation is connected to the city via a pedestrian bridge – a safe, grade-separated

**Cooper, Robertson & Partners 1992**

Lower Manhattan

**Lower Manhattan**

**Cooper, Robertson & Partners 1992**

crossing for students. Designed by Skidmore, Owings & Merrill, this intricate, smart-looking structure is composed of six main elements: a single span, a walkway enclosure, two elevator towers and two sets of stairs. Although plugged into Stuyvesant, it is aesthetically unrelated.

The only eloquent element of the scheme is an art installation commissioned under the auspices of the Department of Cultural Affairs' 'one percent for art' programme. *Mnemonics*, by Kristin Jones and Andrew Ginzel, consists of 400 glass-block reliquaries set at random into the walls of the building.

ADDRESS 345 Chambers Street
CLIENT New York City Board of Education
ASSOCIATE ARCHITECTS Gruzen Samton Steinglass
STRUCTURAL ENGINEER Severud Associates
COST $150 million
SIZE 402,000 square feet (37,350 square metres)
SUBWAY 1, 2, 3, A, C to Chambers Street
BUS M10, M22
ACCESS none

**Cooper, Robertson & Partners 1992**

**Cooper, Robertson & Partners 1992**

# Foley Square Courthouse

Design/build proposals for two federal buildings – a courthouse and an office block (see page 44) – were solicited by the General Services Administration in 1988. During a design/build project, a single entity is responsible for both the design and construction of the job – a popular strategy for the erection of public buildings which can be fast tracked, cutting down on design development time. Developer-led teams of contractors and architects submitted costings and schematic design proposals; following a lengthy selection process, the winning team for the courthouse was Kohn Pedersen Fox with Lehrer McGovern Bovis as core and shell contractor, Structure Tone as interiors contractor and BPT Properties as developer.

One of the largest federal court complexes in the country, set on a wide site in a tight context, the design resolution required a strong awareness of scale. Much thought was given to integrating this skyscraper into its setting and to defining clearly the boundaries between the residential and the civic. A small plaza at the front minimises the spatial impact of the tall structure. The western edge has an internal gallery at ground level that creates a sense of continuity between public spaces.

Taking its height level and formal inspiration from Cass Gilbert's 1936 US Courthouse, the overall style is neo-neo-classical. A formal entrance declaiming conventional ideas about the public realm is echoed compositionally by a top-heavy crown at the apex. The internal composition was worked around a complex narrative. Large courtrooms served by adjunct spaces and judges' chambers had to be matched by accessible support areas. This was partially achieved by placing the courts in a vaulted volume connected to the 410-foot-high tower.

The vertically complex structure has an eccentric triad of circulation systems. Each successive floor alternates judges' chambers and court-

**Lower Manhattan**

**Kohn Pedersen Fox Associates 1995**

**Kohn Pedersen Fox Associates 1995**

rooms. Judges have their own circulation labyrinth which includes private lifts while prisoners are kept to their own corridors including an underground tunnel and sallyports. The public areas encompass circulation, a lobby, a through-block galleria and the oak-lined outdoor plaza.

**Lower Manhattan**

ADDRESS 500 Pearl Street
CLIENT BPT Properties, a joint venture of Bechtel Investments Realty, Inc. and The Park Tower Group
ASSOCIATE ARCHITECTS Simmons Architects
STRUCTURAL ENGINEER The Office of Irwin G Cantor
SIZE 921,000 square feet (85,560 square metres)
SUBWAY 4, 5, 6, J, M to Brooklyn Bridge–City Hall
BUS M1, M9, M10, M15, M22
ACCESS public areas open

**Kohn Pedersen Fox Associates 1995**

Lower Manhattan

**Kohn Pedersen Fox Associates 1995**

# Federal Office Building at Foley Square

This project – by Hellmuth, Obata & Kassabaum with contractors Tishman Foley Partners and developer Linpro New York Realty – was chosen for its commercial merits. The course of action once the job was secured involved simultaneous design development, cost estimates and subcontracting. Erection of the steel structure began while the scheme was still on the drawing board. The developers were responsible for everything from floorplate efficiencies to finding the best utility rebates.

Obviously this is not a method for producing groundbreaking new architecture; unsurprisingly the Federal Office Building is dull but not offensive. Authoritative massing combined with staid grey cladding create a dignified and unobtrusive effect. A curved colonnade at the apex echoes 1920s skyscraper design. Decorative elements give body to the façade – abundant setbacks, recessed cornices, pilasters. The design of the interior arcade had to be altered during construction to avoid an African-American burial ground discovered during excavation. This is now a protected historic site.

The courthouse (see page 40) and office building share a lot in common. Herbert Muschamp, architectural critic for the *New York Times*, aptly titled his critique of the projects, 'A Pair of Towers Trapped in Gray Flannel Suits'. It would be refreshing to see the government commission a building for its innovative design, not its economic virtue.

ADDRESS 290 Broadway
STRUCTURAL ENGINEER Ysrael A Seinuk
COST $276 million SIZE 940,000 square feet (87,300 square metres)
SUBWAY 4, 5, 6, J, M to Brooklyn Bridge–City Hall
BUS M1, M9, M10, M15, M22
ACCESS arcade open

**Lower Manhattan**

**Hellmuth, Obata & Kassabaum 1995**

**Lower Manhattan**

**Hellmuth, Obata & Kassabaum 1995**

# Tribeca and SoHo

In *Civil Architecture: The New Public Infrastructure* (McGraw Hill, 1995), Richard Dattner writes: 'If architects were likened to doctors, architects designing public facilities would be closest to physicians attending emergency rooms – practicing in public view, balancing conflicting requirements first, focusing on essentials, constantly evaluating priorities.' The book's title, a wordplay on civic architecture, reveals Dattner's preoccupation during 30 years of practice. Describing his design convictions, he states, 'Those who design civil architecture labor at the intersection of their culture's aspirations, political struggles and available resources. The realization of civil architecture requires civility, compromise, improvisation, accommodation, patience, tenacity and a sense of humor.'

By claiming that the existence of primary school PS 234 is of greater import than the building itself, Dattner opens the door for critique. Yes, it is admirable that such a work exists, and yes, the building does succeed on many levels. The dichotomy occurs in the comparison of his sophisticated thoughts about public-realm projects and the somewhat quaint, cutesy execution of this particular example.

It is the first public school to be built in New York City for ten years. Notorious for its underfunded school system, the city sponsored a programme to build 12 new schools in which four firms – Gruzen Samton Steinglass, Perkins & Will, Ehrenkrantz & Eckstut Architects and Richard Dattner & Associates Architects – were commissioned to design modular prototypes adaptable to sites throughout Manhattan and the boroughs.

PS 234 sits on a site in TriBeCa which was once flush with the Hudson River. As a result of landfill over the last 100 years the site is now landlocked, bordered by Washington Market Park. The overall form of the

**Richard Dattner Architect 1988**

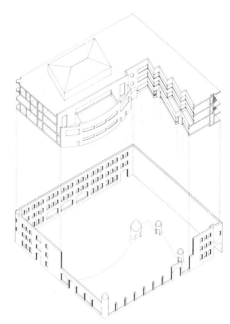

**Tribeca and SoHo**

**Richard Dattner Architect 1988**

three-storey edifice is a serrated rectangle wrapped by a brick courtyard. A maritime theme adds historical rhetoric and four turrets in the courtyard set up the child-scale proportions. These red-brick lighthouses are functional: one houses a reading alcove, two provide access to the courtyard for kindergarteners and the fourth is a bell tower where each day a different student rings the bell.

Worth a separate visit is Intermediate School 218 located at 4600 Broadway and West 96th Street. Another prototype school designed by Dattner in 1993, this project has a great curving façade that serves as an inviting entryway. Architecturally superior, this brick junior high is not quite as twee as PS 234.

ADDRESS Greenwich Street (Warren–Chambers Streets)
STRUCTURAL ENGINEER Goldreich, Page & Thropp
COST $14.5 million
SIZE 75,000 square feet (7000 square metres)
SUBWAY 1, 2, 3, 9, A to Chambers Street; C, E to World Trade Center
BUS M10, M22
ACCESS none

**Richard Dattner Architect 1988**

**Richard Dattner Architect 1988**

**Chelsea Pictures**

The logo for television-commercial production company Chelsea Pictures – a 1940s aeroplane – generated the classically trendy design of its offices. Architect Fred Schwartz produces superb low-budget projects that use practical materials with panache. Other recent work by the firm includes Bumble + Bumble (see page 192) and Provisions, a coffee shop in Union Square. Schwartz was greatly influenced by the late Alan Buchsbaum, architect of the Moon Dance Diner on Sixth Avenue and Grand Street and many other fabulous projects of the 1970s and early 1980s.

The exterior shell of the building was kept intact and the inserted programme – an open production area, three private offices, an enclosed conference room and support spaces – placed on a shifted axis running the building's length. Leaving the elevator one steps on to a stageset complete with green velvet drapery and an oversized amorphic desk whose sandblasted glass top and red naugahyde base foreshadow the ambience and materials of the space beyond. Industrial workbenches are demarcated by off-the-shelf steel-pipe rail and aluminium fittings. These metal elements create a dialogue with maple plywood filing cabinets and the hierarchically placed maple-framed glass executive enclosures.

The artificially skylit box of the freestanding conference area is clad in burgundy naugahyde upholstery. Bank of England chairs surround an elegantly fanciful table covered with 1940s floral linoleum. Aligned with an existing window, an interior strip window allows a peek at the Manhattan skyline.

ADDRESS 122 Hudson Street
COST $200,000 SIZE 2200 square feet (204 square metres)
SUBWAY 1/9 to Franklin Street; A, C, E to Canal Street BUS M10
ACCESS none

**Anderson/Schwartz Architects 1994**

Tribeca and SoHo

**Anderson/Schwartz Architects 1994**

**Nobu**

A collaboration between restaurateur Drew Nieporent, world-class chef Nobu Matsuhisa and actor Robert De Niro, this is currently one of the coolest locations in Manhattan. The epitome of silly pretentiousness, it takes several weeks to get a Friday-night table reservation – unless, of course, you are a friend of the proprietor or, even better, a celebrity.

The space is melodramatic. Architect David Rockwell states that in approaching projects his conceptual glue is 'architecture as theater'. Nobu resembles architecture as soap opera.

The open sequence of spaces (the site was originally a bank) was inspired by rural Japan's mountainous landscape. A rich palette of materials is used to differentiate horizontal and vertical surfaces. The high ceiling is emphasised by three real birch trunks containing lighting topped by rusted steel plates which sprout scorched ashwood branches, spreading ethereal shadows on the ceiling. Red cherry blossoms resembling fallen flowers are stencilled on the floor.

Adorable chopstick chairs at the sushi bar display Rockwell's witty style. The surrounding gently curved freestanding walls are sushi shaped and extravagantly finished: thousands of shiny black stones have been embedded into one; gold-leaf polka dots drift across another. Lighting sconces that resemble duelling samurai swords are interspersed with sound-absorption panels that resemble parchment scrolls. The food is as theatrically designed as the space.

ADDRESS 105 Hudson Street
COST $1 million SIZE 2800 square feet (260 square metres)
SUBWAY 1/9 to Franklin Street; A, C, E to Canal Street
BUS M10
ACCESS open

**Rockwell Group 1994**

**Rockwell Group 1994**

# El Teddy's

A full-size replica of the Statue of Liberty's crown rests atop this Mexican restaurant. Underneath is an organic purple, orange, green and yellow glass-mosaic canopy. An eclectic hybrid of multi-textural iconography, this project is essentially an exploration of surfaces.

The site has been a restaurant since the 1920s. Two adjoining three-storey brick buildings were originally known as Teddy's. The restaurant was reinvented as El Internacional in the early 1980s. Designed by artist Antoni Miralda, El Internacional was a small piece of a larger artwork, the *Honeymoon Project*, an international series of installations celebrating the marriage of the Statue of Liberty to Christopher Columbus (one of the most memorable of these was the *Statue of Liberty's Wedding Dress* – made actual size – hung in the Winter Garden of the World Financial Center).

Purchased and redesigned by Christopher Chesnutt in 1989, the restaurant has been reincarnated through a strategy of stripping and layering exemplified by its name, a combination of elements of its two previous lives. The split-level plan and circulation were left intact while wall coverings and decorative elements were peeled away and then added to. Chesnutt assiduously avoided clichéd references to a 'Mexican look', the single subtle homage towards the cuisine served being a vintage fabric wall covering dotted with sombreros in one of the dining spaces.

Chesnutt enlisted the services of several craft artists who created their work on site. The Gaudi-like form of the exterior canopy was shaped as it was built out of steel, wire mesh, silicone and stained glass. The mosaicist then created patterns directly across this structure, a reception desk, a grand chandelier and a mirror. The mirrors in the hallway, constructed of old chair parts and picture frames, include elements found on site. An exercise in recycling (before its time), the interior stair railing is a

**Christopher Chesnutt 1989**

**Christopher Chesnutt 1989**

delightful combination of welded forks, cash-register components, existing railing and burners from the old stove. A neon installation glows underneath the Lucite staircase. Ornate and elaborate, the project has an appealing feel of a work in progress.

Chesnutt also designed a restaurant next door: Layla at 211 West Broadway.

ADDRESS 219 West Broadway
SIZE 7000 square feet (650 square metres)
SUBWAY 1/9 to Franklin Street
BUS M6, M10
ACCESS open

**Christopher Chesnutt 1989**

**Christopher Chesnutt 1989**

# Lehmann Maupin Gallery

One's first reaction to this brand-new space is disappointment – much ado about nothing. Located smack in the centre of SoHo's contemporary art corridor, this capacious gallery is celebrity architect Rem Koolhaas' only realised project to date in New York, though his book *Delirious New York* – a delightfully zany manifesto on Manhattan's urban condition first published in 1978 – is still a must-read for city buffs.

The objective of the gallery was to create a dialogue between the artwork and the space. Co-founder David Maupin describes their collaborative intentions: 'Rather than opening another gallery in the traditional sense, we wanted ours to be a work/space – something closer to an artist's studio. The environment we created is extremely adaptable to a variety of needs, including exhibition space, private showroom, and office.'

Organised around a set of massive sliding/hanging walls, the space has the potential to be reconfigured in several ways. Visually noisier than the Richard Gluckman white cubes of the 1980s (see page 66), this is not an ideologically neutral space: the modular plywood floors and ceilings are chock-a-block with cyberwiring and industrial light fixtures.

The permanently temporary nature of the gallery leads one to wonder how the Lehmann Maupin will transform over time. Will mnemonic reminders be left of each successive exhibition? Perhaps after a series of different shows the subtle versatility of the architectural design will be more readable.

ADDRESS 39 Greene Street
SUBWAY 6, C to Spring Street; B, D, F, Q to Broadway/Lafayette; N, R to Prince Street
BUS M1, M5, M6, M21
ACCESS open

Tribeca and SoHo

**Rem Koolhaas 1996**

**Tribeca and SoHo**

**Rem Koolhaas 1996**

**Bar 89**

The undoubtable *pièce de résistance* of this bar/restaurant is its provacative unisex loo. Customers in the know make a conspicuous beeline through the eatery and up the stairs to the mirrored bathroom area. Five stall doors that transform from transparent to opaque when occupied await the brave patron. Made from clear glass with a liquid-crystal core, the doors are activated by motion sensors. Once inside, the stall feels quite private and secure. This gimmicky gesture is amusing and the use of new materials much appreciated.

The 1990s aesthetic of these bathrooms carries through into the architectural bones of this brand-new building in the carefully preserved Cast Iron District of SoHo. Views and light, the contrast of transparent and translucent, were the driving concepts behind the design. The minimalist modernist façade is clean, unexpectedly using curved glass to great effect. The double-height interior is lit by a 40-foot-long skylight abutting the side wall. A switchback granite and steel staircase winds dramatically up to a mezzanine-level lounge, the hierarchy ending at the washrooms.

This modern skeleton is sadly diminished by the dated, cringe-making 1980s black-leather and metal furnishings, black banquette and single vase flower display.

ADDRESS 89 Mercer Street
CLIENT NY 93 Corp
ASSOCIATE DESIGNERS Janis Leonard Design Associates
STRUCTURAL ENGINEER Hage Engineering
SIZE 4975 square feet (462 square metres)
SUBWAY 6, C to Spring Street; B, D, F, Q to Broadway/Lafayette; N, R to Prince Street BUS M1, M5, M6, M21
ACCESS open

**Ogawa/Depardon 1995**

**130 Prince Street**

This po-mo addition to SoHo is clearly trying to stay in keeping with its surroundings. Well constructed and immediately identifiable as new, it is the epitome of poorly sited retro art deco. (Commercial projects in New York seem to have a propensity for a neo-art-deco look that is difficult to comprehend.) Pink granite, green trim, concrete and sanded lilac-tinted aluminium create an unwelcomely pretty exterior. This project lacks the grittiness downtown New York is renowned for. Once a bakery, the ground level is now home to Nicole Miller and Omari shops.

ADDRESS 130 Prince Street
ASSOCIATE ARCHITECT Walter B Melvin
SUBWAY 6, C to Spring Street; B, D, F, Q to Broadway/Lafayette; N, R to Prince Street
BUS M1, M5, M6, M21
ACCESS retail open

**Lee Manners & Associates 1988**

Tribeca and SoHo

**Lee Manners & Associates 1988**

**Gagosian Gallery**

The well-articulated Gagosian Gallery was a trend-setter for the now-familiar reductive conversion of industrial space into posh gallery space. Designed by Richard Gluckman (best known for his 1987 completion of the Dia Center at 548 West 22nd Street), this is a near-perfect setting for large contemporary sculpture. Created with the work of Richard Serra in mind, the elegantly neutral space is light, airy and capacious. Gluckman believes that the art should dominate the space, with the architect in a supporting role, merely creating a backdrop. He describes himself as an 'expeditor for the artist, not a collaborator'.

Only the 12-foot brick façade of the original garage was left untouched. A new garage door was added, both historical homage and practical facility. This vast entry is left open in summer; on early summer evenings the gallery glows enticingly, offering passers-by more than a glimpse of what is on display.

The gallery's interior envelope was completely redesigned: the floor was reinforced, the ceiling was raised to maximum height, and a pier-and-wall structure was instituted to increase the width. The cracked-concrete floor, burnished and smooth, contrasts beautifully with the brilliant white walls. Gluckman has left exposed beams that correspond to the existing foundation structure, visible in the new skylights. Aside from natural light, fixed-point industrial halogen light fixtures are ceiling mounted around the circumference of the skylights.

ADDRESS 136 Wooster Street
STRUCTURAL ENGINEEER Ross Dalland
SUBWAY 6, C to Spring Street; B, D, F, Q to Broadway/Lafayette; N, R to Prince Street BUS M1, M5, M6, M21
ACCESS open

**Richard Gluckman 1994**

**Richard Gluckman 1994**

**The Guggenheim Museum SoHo**

The Guggenheim expanded to this site in 1992, cashing in on the thriving SoHo art scene. In a strategy perilously close to that of a retail chain, the new branch provides the museum with a presence within the wider context of the city. But the 'Downtown Guggenheim' offers a different product from the uptown outlet: through a corporate relationship with the German telecommunications carrier Deutsche Telekom, the space is in the first phase of its development as a state-of-the-art multi-media museum devoted to electronics-oriented exhibits.

Designed and redesigned by Arata Isozaki, the museum is an odd mix of minimalist elegance and tacky, pseudo-high tech. Although Isozaki has now been able to complete his original scheme, I preferred the museum's initial incarnation: minimalist and serene. Housed in the shell of a cast-iron commercial structure dating back to 1882, the six-storey building boasts the largest floorplates (100 feet wide by 200 feet long) in the neighbourhood. The upper galleries are open loft spaces with bleached white-oak floors and an elegant rhythm of columns. The new facilities, concentrated on the ground floor, include interactive virtual-reality stations and a 14- by 51-foot video wall. This floor has been taken over by a mock-industrial look that tries too hard. The 'dumbing' of the Guggenheim's programme has had a diminishing effect on its architecture.

ADDRESS 575 Broadway
ASSOCIATE ARCHITECT TAS Design
STRUCTURAL ENGINEER Gilsanz Murray Steficek
COST $6 million SIZE 40,000 square feet (3700 square metres)
SUBWAY 6, C to Spring Street; B, D, F, Q to Broadway/Lafayette; N, R to Prince Street BUS M1, M5, M6, M21
ACCESS open

**Arata Isozaki & Associates 1996**

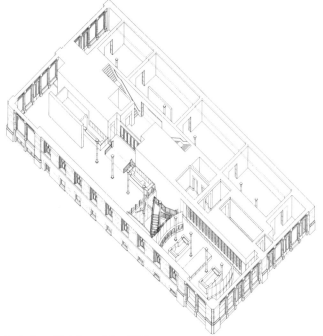

**Arata Isozaki & Associates 1996**

**Museum for African Art**

SoHo became the heart of New York's contemporary art scene following the area's decline as an industrial and commercial centre. Since the 1960s artists have moved into abandoned warehouses and avant-garde boutiques and galleries are continually springing up. In the last decade three museums – the Guggenheim Museum SoHo (see page 68), the New Museum for Contemporary Art and the Museum for African Art – have established sites along Broadway, creating a mini Museum Row.

The Museum for African Art is essentially a loft conversion. Maya Lin is best known as the designer of the Vietnam Veterans Memorial in Washington DC and her sculptural approach has enhanced the otherwise straightforward concept. A copper-pipe statue based on an African symbol for humanity heralds the entrance. The space is intended to be experienced as a narrative journey from the front to the back, down a dark staircase and up a bright golden staircase. The irregular curves for the stairs – the building's best feature – were drawn freehand on site. Colour also plays a large part in creating the museum's texture: the floor is a stained bluish-green timber and the walls are grey, blue and gold.

Lin recently created the installation *Eclipsed Time* in the newly renovated Penn Station (see page 118).

ADDRESS 593 Broadway
SIZE 12,500 square feet (1160 square metres)
SUBWAY 6 to Bleecker Street; B, D, F, Q to Broadway/Lafayette; N, R to Prince Street
BUS M1, M5, M6, M21
ACCESS open

**Maya Lin and David Hotson 1993**

**Maya Lin and David Hotson 1993**

**Time Out New York**

London listings magazine *Time Out* sets out to be 'irreverent, comprehensive and independent'. The New York edition is not quite as sparky, but the design of its downtown headquarters makes up for it.

Situated in a fashionable, post-industrial district known as NoHo, the space exudes a gritty urban personality. Designers Margaret Helfand and Marti Cowan describe their objectives as: 'To explore new approaches to generating form, organizing space and constructing. Specific functional and structural requirements are reduced to their basic components and then become the expressive language of each project. Forms, frequently irregular and unexpected, are generated by context, program requirements or method of construction.'

Here nothing is orthogonal. Angles abound. Iconoclastic materials float in the air, meeting at unexpected intersections to create unusual spaces. Only the wooden strip floor and freshly painted white walls of the gutted interior – recognisable elements of an archetypal loft conversion – were left intact. Helfand and Cowan's plan, commissioned and executed within 12 weeks, nimbly departs from the typical.

A streetwise, full-height metal chainlink fence of the type usually found at the perimeter of inner-city basketball courts greets the visitor stepping out of the elevator, allowing visibility but not easy access. Skewed planes of translucent corrugated-fibreglass panels and strand board partitions stained with bronze and aluminium dust are visible through the mesh.

An off-centre hallway organises the plan. This is demarcated by a wavy, ridged-fibreglass wall running the length of the space. This transparent divider is punctuated only to allow circulation into the individual work areas. Skewed angles and triangular forms are visible overhead as requirements for air, light and networking develop into elements of informal geometry.

**Margaret Helfand Architects 1995**

**Margaret Helfand Architects 1995**

The odd, unresolved angles make tight quarters feel more capacious. Helfand explains her strategy: 'The hallway is contained and a big move visually, allowing other elements to fade into the background and creating a combination of cacophony and control. Slight disorientation disconnects the inhabitant from feeling like a sardine in a can.'

Prefabricated computer workstations for 70 users were designed as an elegant kit of parts. Constructed of composite panels of strand board and tectum tack surface – an insulation material usually hidden on the under layer in construction – they can be arranged in flexible clusters to form interchangeable rooms. Private offices at several perimeter locations allow light transmission to the interior through fibreglass partitions. These are inexpensive materials used with wit.

One of Helfand's most refreshing preoccupations is the use of materials in their pure state. The palette at *Time Out* is neutral, the only nod to colour being the bronze dust and the postcards, clippings, Polaroids, books and personal objects that enliven each workstation. The play of light filtered through the fibreglass creates natural colour. Furniture and accessories – the granite reception desk, rubber adjustable chairs, filing cabinets and wastebins – are all jet black except for the strategically placed Isamu Noguchi paper lamps. And, of course, most of the staff are stylishly dressed in black.

ADDRESS 7th Floor, 627 Broadway
COST $216,000
SIZE 8000 square feet (740 square metres)
SUBWAY 6 to Bleecker Street; B, D, F, Q to Broadway/Lafayette; N, R to Prince Street BUS M1, M5, M6, M21
ACCESS none

**Margaret Helfand Architects 1995**

Tribeca and SoHo

**Margaret Helfand Architects 1995**

**Storefront for Art & Architecture**

The relationship between art and architecture (and specifically architecture as art) continues to be an issue for debate. The imaginary dividing line is excruciatingly elastic, mutating with the whims of fashion and avant-garde theory. The Storefront for Art & Architecture stands both as a work of art and a functional space. Displayed as an object, the building itself was the exhibit in the project's first months of existence.

Storefront occupies a tiny pie-shaped slice of Manhattan. Categorised as an alternative, non-profit-making space, it is devoted to the consideration of the city as a work of art. A reportedly not altogether happy design collaboration between architect Steven Holl and artist Vito Acconci, the intention is to promote public interaction. Blurring the boundaries between street and building, the small space and its surroundings merge so that inside and outside begin to become one and the same.

The concrete board façade is composed of irregular, rectilinear plates that fit together like a jigsaw puzzle. In warm weather these plates revolve from pivot points and can be adjusted by the public into varying states of openness. Founder Kyong Park describes the idea as 'Pop architecture; cheap, iconic and dispensable, the merchandising of an idea and experience.' Even the name embodies the idea of culture as a commodity in a snub to the often snooty New York art world.

Powerful in concept but flimsy in detailing, it is a fantastic project.

ADDRESS 97 Kenmare Street
CLIENT Kyong Park and Shirin Neshat, Storefront for Art & Architecture
COST $80,000 SIZE 1026 square feet (95.3 square metres)
SUBWAY 6 to Spring Street; B, D, F, Q to Broadway/Lafayette; J, M to
Bowery BUS M1, M103
ACCESS open

**Tribeca and SoHo**

**Steven Holl and Vito Acconci 1993**

**Steven Holl and Vito Acconci 1993**

# West Village, Greenwich Village, East Village

**Industria Superstudio**

A fashionable architect who works within the fashion world, Deborah Berke has developed her own brand of minimalism. Industria, a fashion-photography superstudio designed for Fabrizio Ferri, is a fine example of her supersubtle design process.

Not much is going on here, but then not much needs to. The space is about background, flexibility, the creation of a neutral stageset for photo shoots. Berke has left much of the original fabric of the former Rolls-Royce repair garage intact, and concrete floors, cinderblock walls, visible ductwork and empty surfaces pretty much describe the space.

This is non-design design. Berke's aesthetic goal is to create an invisible architecture, a generic architecture. Streamlined and clean, it looks very ordinary, but on close inspection it proves to be a calculated ordinariness. Pretty invisible and pretty generic.

ADDRESS 775 Washington Street
SIZE 20,000 square feet (1900 square metres)
SUBWAY A, C, E, L to 14th Street
BUS M11, M14
ACCESS none

**West Village, Greenwich Village, East Village**

**Deborah Berke 1991**

**Deborah Berke 1991**

# Washington Court

The most interesting aspect of this rather straightforward residential and retail complex was the reaction of the vocal local community. Though Polshek's proposal was site sensitive and contextual – and he himself lived almost next door – the neighbourhood was outraged. The Greenwich Village Historic District is notorious for its strict preservation codes, and residents felt a building that mirrored the nearby 1834 Greek revival church of St Joseph would be more appropriate. A heated public debate ensued, but after a lengthy stalemate and changing of the guard, the end result was a building constructed almost exactly as initially offered.

Twenty-four duplex condos, four single-storey penthouses and 25,000 square feet of commercial space are housed behind a six-storey, three-bay, red-brick, limestone and terracotta façade designed to echo the surrounding brick row houses. The white concrete and steel rear façade was inspired by Mies van der Rohe's Weissenhofsiedlung in Stuttgart.

The design presented an interesting technical problem. The architects felt it was important to maintain the Sixth Avenue street wall, but this placed the front of the building on top of subway and sewer lines. The solution was to cantilever the first 20 feet of the complex over these underground tunnels from columns placed mid-block. Compressable neoprene pads were incorporated to deaden the roar of the subway.

ADDRESS Sixth Avenue between Waverly Place and Washington Place
CLIENT Philips International Holding Corp.
STRUCTURAL ENGINEER Andrew Elliott & Associates
COST $9.5 million SIZE 67,500 square feet (6270 square metres)
SUBWAY 1/9 to Christopher Street; A, B, C, D, E, F, Q to West 4th Street
BUS M5, M6, M8
ACCESS none

**James Stewart Polshek and Partners Architects 1986**

**West Village, Greenwich Village, East Village**

**James Stewart Polshek and Partners Architects 1986**

# Hetrick Martin Institute

'There's no there there,' claims Smith-Miller + Hawkinson. 'The project was designed so as to present the visitor with multiple points of view. The use of transparency allows for vision to traverse the different programmatic divisions. The design allows for programmatically discrete spaces whose boundaries can be shifted to create a blurring of functional zones.'

This is a superb illustration of socially conscious architecture, of deinstitutionalising an institution. Hetrick Martin is a non-profit-making social services, education and advocacy organisation for gay and lesbian youth. Three main programmes were intertwined in this Greenwich Village loft: the Harvey Milk High School; Project First Step, a street outreach programme for homeless adolescents; and the Drop-In Center.

The space empowers the visitor by intensified visibility. Upon arriving at the main reception area one can see through glass or transparent Lexan plastic to the administrative departments and beyond to the windows. A non-gridded plan, with all spatial divisions set slightly askew, combined with the architects' trademark sliding walls/doors provides flexibility. An inexpensive palette of unfinished materials – maple fin plywood, aluminium, Homasote and blackboard paint (the reception area has an entire wall coated with this material to emphasise the act of communication) – cost $40 per square foot. The kids have added their own touches, painting walls lemon and hanging purple drapery. Overhead ducts, sprinklers and lighting are visible – nothing here is concealed.

ADDRESS 2 Astor Place
STRUCTURAL ENGINEER Severud Associates
SUBWAY 6 to Astor Place; N, R to 8th Street
BUS M1, M2, M3, M8, M101, M102, M103
ACCESS none

**Smith-Miller + Hawkinson Architects 1994**

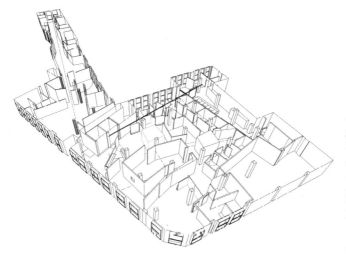

**Smith-Miller + Hawkinson Architects 1994**

# Cooper Union Residence Hall

The design for this historically contextual project followed three main principles: the synthesis of 19th- and 20th-century geometries, the accommodation of existing zoning codes and the notion of campus.

Overlapping grids dictated the building's square and rectangular massing. In reality three separate intersecting structures, the overall volumetric character is rational and cohesive. The expression of old and new is achieved through the varying widths of the layered frontage: narrow strips retain the character of the neighbourhood while the wider street wall of the high-rise tower looks more contemporary.

The location creates a triangle between the school, the dorm and a statue of Tom Thumb. The interior is intended as an internal campus with private space leading on to public areas. The masterplan offers loftlike two-bedroom apartments (four per floor), ceremonial rooms and common space. Generous windows create a light, airy interior.

Aesthetically unexceptional, this well-organised and unobtrusive red-brick building was the result of a competition involving 11 invited architects. The three finalists were all Cooper Union graduates: Peter Eisenman, Diane Lewis and Rolf Olhausen. A year and a half of debate ensued before Prentice & Chan, Olhausen was given the commission.

The adjacent School of Architecture, erected in 1859, was designed by Frederick A Peterson. The oldest existing building framed with steel beams in the US, it is a National Landmark. The elegant interior was reconstructed in 1975 by dean of the School of Architecture John Hejduk.

ADDRESS Third Avenue and Stuyvesant Place
SUBWAY 6 to Astor Place; N, R to 8th Street
BUS M1, M2, M3, M8, M101, M102, M103
ACCESS commercial ground-floor level open

**Prentice & Chan, Olhausen 1992**

West Village, Greenwich Village, East Village

**Prentice & Chan, Olhausen 1992**

# Union Square

**Zeckendorf Towers**

Union Square, originally known as Union Place, has undergone numerous transformations. Union Place evolved as a result of being the junction where Broadway, the post road to Albany and the post road to Boston (now Third Avenue) met. Before the Civil War the neighbourhood was grand and fashionable, home to many exclusive stores and theatres. In 1811 the plan for Manhattan's streets to be organised as a Cartesian grid was set into motion. Since Broadway cut a southeast–northwest slash across the city, squares were created wherever Broadway hit a north–south avenue. Union Square, Gramercy Park, Stuyvesant Square and Madison Square were developments reminiscent of London's many Georgian squares.

In 1936 the park was relandscaped and raised several feet above ground to accommodate the new subway. After the war Union Square became a public gathering spot for the political left and many rallies and labour demonstrations were held there. The area gradually deteriorated and by the 1970s the park was drug ridden, an ugly haven for junkies and their suppliers.

In 1986 the city renovated the park, removing all perimeter foliage to allow visibility from the street. Art-deco-inspired steel and glass kiosks were added above the subway entrance together with a matching newsstand. Mundane in design, these elements were nevertheless successful in turning round the park's atmosphere. Today Union Square is once again on the up and trendy restaurants and cafés are popping up around the square. A Farmers Market was instituted in 1976 by the New York City Planning Department and the Council on the Environment to entice shoppers to the area. A fine example of the power of an architecture of event, this greenmarket has been a terrific success.

The provision of high-end residential properties was initially consid-

**Union Square**

**Davis, Brody & Associates 1987**

**Davis, Brody & Associates 1987**

ered to be a key to the area's gentrification and Zeckendorf Towers was the first development to be erected with this objective in mind. The large mixed-use building covers a full block bound by East 14th and 15th Streets, Irving Place and Union Square East. Curiously, however, the project turns its back on Union Square. Four towers containing 675 apartments are placed above an eight-storey rectilinear structure housing offices and shops. Life in the towers is not only self-contained (shopping facilities and a private health club can be reached from within), but the entrance to all the apartments is from 15th Street – far removed from the square. A process of negotiation between the city, the client and the community led to the commercial plinth, but the overscaled design does nothing to make Union Square a more inviting setting. The Con Edison Tower clockface is blocked from most vantage points in the park and rather than making the square seem more intimate and inviting, the towers merely add an element of exclusive seclusion hovering above.

The project's aesthetic is an unusual diversion for Davis, Brody & Associates. Vaguely post-modern, heavy and ugly, the edifice seems too large for its site. The glowing floating pyramids perched atop the towers redeem the building somewhat at night, but even then the oppressive overall massing is troublesome.

ADDRESS 1 Irving Place
CLIENT Zeckendorf Company
STRUCTURAL ENGINEER Rosenwasser Grossman
COST $120 million
SUBWAY 4, 5, 6, L, N, R to 14th Street/Union Square
BUS M1, M2, M3, M6, M7
ACCESS commercial space open

**Union Square**

**Davis, Brody & Associates 1987**

Union Square

**Davis, Brody & Associates 1987**

**City Bakery**

City Bakery can be classified as classical post-urban minimalist. The architects have manipulated a low budget and awkward industrial space with irony and wit. Industrial elements appear in unexpected configurations: coat hooks are large metal bolts, magazine holders are galvanised-steel ducts. The daily menu is a roll of hanging butchers' paper. A wall of symmetrically placed white cake boxes is chic Japanese simplicity with a New York twist. Circular benches and fixed tables with revolving satellite seats on wheels are precursors of Turett's Newsbar stools (see page 96). Intended as an architectural analogue to the exquisite cakes served on the premises, the space is as simply elegant as owner/chef Maury Rubin's tarts.

**Union Square**

ADDRESS 22 East 17th Street
SIZE 1800 square feet (170 square metres)
SUBWAY 4, 5, 6, L, N, R to 14th Street/Union Square
BUS M1, M2, M3, M6, M7
ACCESS open

**Turett Freyer Collaborative Architects 1991**

**Turett Freyer Collaborative Architects 1991**

**Newsbar**

Wayne Turett, principal designer of Newsbar, obviously delights in sophisticated spaces. Earlier projects include a post-modern news-stand on the Upper West Side and City Bakery (see page 94).

Set in the Flatiron district, this is the first of three coffee bars dotted around downtown Manhattan (other locations are 366 West Broadway and 107 University Place). Designed before the city suffered a plethora of bland brand coffee vendors on every corner, Newsbar is gritty glamour. Citified, urbane, almost blasé, these are coffee bars to be seen in.

A rough concrete envelope faced with floor-to-ceiling glass creates an energetic dialogue with the street. Televisions mounted above the service counter are visible from the sidewalk, enhancing the physicality of the interior/exterior conversation. There is seating for 12, plenty of window standing room and outdoor benches, so activity spills out on to the street.

An array of some 500 magazines and periodicals offsets the industrial elements. The innovative use of mundane materials is quite lively. The service counter is enclosed with translucent fibreglass. Galvanised sheet metal and guy wires are used for the pivoting journal-display racks which are conceptually intended to imitate information flow, Newsbar's primary programme. Custom satellite tables fabricated out of raw steel spin round fixed central supports. The tabletops feature glossy magazines sealed under glass. Très New York.

**Union Square**

ADDRESS 2 West 19th Street
STRUCTURAL ENGINEER Stan Gleit
SIZE 600 square feet (56 square metres)
SUBWAY F, N, R to 23rd Street
BUS M2, M3, M5, M6, M7
ACCESS open

**Turett Collaborative Architects 1991**

Union Square

**Turett Collaborative Architects 1991**

**JSM Music Studios**

Gisue and Mojgan Hariri describe their vision of this funky space as 'the movement of breath through a trumpet'. Compositionally combining curvilinear (melodic) and rectilinear (rhythmic) elements, an intertwined relationship between space, materials and inhabitation occurs.

The raw loft space was originally 10,000 square feet but once the recording studios were in place – a series of jagged, wonky enclosures mapped out by an acoustician – the Hariris were left with only 4500 square feet in which to insert the rest of the programme.

As you step out of the elevator, a colourful hologram of the JSM logo (designed by artist Rudie Berkhout) shimmers seductively in a steel window frame. On entering the reception area a view of the columned corridor is offset by three blue cushions perched on an elliptical black bench – an over-cutesy representation of musical notation. The cerulean and beige lounge is dominated by a curving steel screen shielding the stairway. Brushed steel and metal mesh appear unexpectedly as ceiling elements and a swish stainless-steel kitchen can be glimpsed in the corner.

This project alternates between dynamic architectonic gestures and silly decoration. Custom-designed furniture – blue-cushioned barstools, coffee tables made of discarded subway grating, jutting marble wall ledges – adds syncopation to the jazzy rhythm of the floor layout.

ADDRESS 59 West 19th Street
ARCHITECT OF RECORD Michael Berzak
STRUCTURAL ENGINEER Robert Silman Associates
SIZE 4500 square feet (420 square metres)
SUBWAY 1/9 to 18th Street; B, D, Q to 14th Street; F to 23rd Street
BUS M5, M6, M7
ACCESS none

**Union Square**

**Hariri & Hariri 1992**

**Union Square**

**Hariri & Hariri 1992**

# Turtle Bay and Murray Hill

# Skirball Institute of Biomolecular Medicine

Three programmes were fitted into this well-organised complex: the ground floor is the primary entrance to the entire NYU medical complex, the lower five storeys are devoted to biomolecular research laboratories and the remaining 20 storeys are faculty offices and staff residences. Implanted between two existing structures, the building completes the lopsided four-block urban campus whose facilities include the NYU Medical School, Tisch Hospital, the Arnold and Marie Schwarz Health Care Center and the Rusk Institute of Rehabilitation Medicine. The unplanned configuration of modernist brick structures built between 1957 and 1976 (designed by Skidmore, Owings & Merrill and Perkins & Will) needed to be made into a cohesive, readable whole. The architects cleverly positioned the new facility to serve several purposes: central entrance, directional connector and wall to an internal courtyard.

The main lobby, entered under a streamlined aluminium and glass canopy, is 16,800 square feet. Double-height, light and airy, it serves as a welcoming entrance to the hospital and medical school. The linking structure to the north is most fun – an oblong, curvilinear glass and aluminium anthropomorphic appendage that wittily accommodates the 4000-square-foot admissions and waiting area for the hospital. The rest of the architectural design is fairly straightforward. Exterior massing hints at the different programmatic functions through the use of different materials: the lab floors are flame-finished granite and the residential floors brick. Granite, aluminium, glass and brick also begin to express the structural bay system.

The circulation for the lab floors is organised along a double-loaded corridor. Each module is divided into a bench area and desk zone on the outer wall and a support zone along the corridor, creating a further circu-

**James Stewart Polshek and Partners Architects 1992**

lation corridor down the middle. The lab floors were kept as shallow as possible to take maximum advantage of daylight. This principle was applied to the faculty medical offices as well, where four suites to a floor are arranged with as much fenestration as possible, creating pleasant, sunshine-filled waiting rooms.

**Turtle Bay and Murray Hill**

ADDRESS 550 First Avenue
CONSULTING ARCHITECT Payette Associates
STRUCTURAL ENGINEER Severud Associates
SIZE 550,000 square feet (51,000 square metres)
SUBWAY 4, 5, 6, S to Grand Central; 7, B, D, F, Q to 42nd Street
BUS M1, M2, M3, M4, M42, M104
ACCESS lobby open

**James Stewart Polshek and Partners Architects 1992**

**Turtle Bay and Murray Hill**

**James Stewart Polshek and Partners Architects 1992**

# The Pierpont Morgan Library

A well-intentioned addition, this enclosed garden court falls just short of success. The courtyard links four disparate structures: the library, designed by Charles McKim in 1906; a 1928 neo-classical annex; J P Morgan's 19th-century Renaissance revival Pierpont Mansion; and a five-storey office block.

The new connecting glass and painted-steel atrium rises 54 feet to a wriggling asymmetrical glass ceiling – an attempt to marry the disparate heights of the mansion and the library. This wave is echoed throughout in both the vertical and horizontal planes. A freestanding 55-foot-long truss stabilised by pretensioned cables and set on steel-jacketed columns apparently supports the majority of the new structure. Although the exterior is visually powerful, the interior – replete with olive trees and climbing fig vines – seems sterile and artificial. There is an excess of dead space: benches sit in a narrow corridor facing an inaccessible outdoor courtyard; a lift opens on to a curved terrace looking down on a passageway, and so on.

The structural system is partially visible, imparting an out-of-place industrial element. One interior elevation – a large and elegant limestone wall inscribed with donors' names – makes one wish more care had been taken with the materials palette. Clear glass, pewter-clad aluminium panels and mullions juxtaposed with the grey and white marble floors bestow an ambience more appropriate to an office-tower lobby.

ADDRESS 29 East 36th Street
STRUCTURAL ENGINEER Weidlinger Associates
SUBWAY 6 to 33rd Street; B, D, F, N, R to 34th Street
BUS M1, M2, M3, M4, M16, M34, Q32
ACCESS open

**Voorsanger Associates 1992**

**Voorsanger Associates 1992**

# Business and Science Library

The New York Public Library, client of this major midtown project, states that it is: 'dedicated to the ideal of placing a comprehensive archive of human thought and achievement at the service of any inquisitive mind'. Here, up to 3000 inquisitive minds can locate entrepreneurial, scientific and technical information in what was once a department store – B Altman's – designed by Trowbridge & Livingstone in 1906. Due to landmark regulations, the current inhabitants did not change the exterior, merely sprucing up the 8-foot-thick exterior walls.

Reconfiguring the interior and challenging traditional notions of civic space, Gwathmey Siegel made the basement level completely public. One enters into the 33-foot-high Healy Hall, a calculated architectural composition made up of four elements: elevator, mezzanine balcony, curved staircase and mural of quotations. The volumetric quality of these interior objects adds a cohesiveness to the redistributed floor levels.

A collection of 1.6 million books required the insertion of two extra floors. After much research, the architects and client concluded that books as objects are still very much an active part of our culture and must be accommodated. So though 100 computer workstations are available, users can still come into direct contact with the printed page.

ADDRESS Madison Avenue and East 34th Street
STRUCTURAL ENGINEER Severud Associates
COST $100 million
SIZE 250,000 square feet (23,000 square metres)
SUBWAY 6 to 33rd Street; B, D, F, N, R to 34th Street
BUS M1, M2, M3, M4, M16, M34, Q32
ACCESS open

**Gwathmey Siegel & Associates Architects 1996**

Turtle Bay and Murray Hill

**Turtle Bay and Murray Hill**

**Gwathmey Siegel & Associates Architects 1996**

**Morgans**

The snootiest of Ian Schrager and Steve Rubell's hotels (see pages 126 and 128), there is no signage outside Morgans. You have to be in the know even to locate this hotel. The elegant 1920s façade was discovered behind a white marble addition probably done in the 1960s. Cleaned, redetailed and reclad, the triple-arched elevation is understated grace.

The proprietors hired chic Parisian designer Andrée Putnam – well known for her discreetly luxurious taste and the only licensed manufacturer and distributor (Ecart International) of furniture and carpets by Eileen Gray and Robert Mallet-Stevens – to do the interiors. The subtle entrance opens on to a small lobby with a *trompe-l'oeil* floor that sets up a three-dimensional interplay between checkered granite and an illusory checkered carpet. Bronze mullions bounce light off the glass walls, adding to the dizzying effect.

The building had previously housed the Executive Hotel, a venue of dubious reputation, and the floor plan of relatively small rooms was not changed. Putnam therefore concentrated on surface treatments: the 154 rooms are primarily grey with marvellous maple furniture sitting on Eileen Gray rugs, of course. The bathrooms have been much publicised. Black and white chessboard tiles, stainless-steel surgical sinks and gigantic shower doors were the ultimate in urban chic when the hotel opened in the mid 1980s.

ADDRESS 237 Madison Avenue
CLIENTS Steve Rubell, Ian Schrager, Philip Pilevsky
COST $4.5 million
SUBWAY 4, 5, 6, 7, S to Grand Central
BUS M1, M2, M3, M4, M42, M104
ACCESS lobby open

Turtle Bay and Murray Hill

**Haigh Space Architects and Andrée Putnam 1985**

**Haigh Space Architects and Andrée Putnam 1985**

# Theater and Garment Districts

# Jacob K Javits Convention Center

'The Center of the World' announces signage on the Jacob Javits Convention Center. Oddly off-centre in relation to New York City's overall programmatic plan, this is a vast, colossal, monstrous, gigantic structure.

Planned as the largest American convention centre contained under one roof, it is in fact the third-largest such facility. Its 21.9-acre site stretches five city blocks and the 18-acre building, its scale that of an international airport terminal, is triple the size of the New York Coliseum, which it replaces in function. Comprising 1.6 million square feet of total functioning area, 720,000 square feet of exhibition space including one hall of 410,000 square feet – reputed to be large enough to house the Statue of Liberty – it can accommodate 85,000 people. In addition to offices, storage and service areas, kitchen and dining facilities and shops there are over 100 private meeting rooms.

The centre sits in a principally residential and underutilised industrial landfill neighbourhood previously occupied by open railyards: Hell's Kitchen (see page 138). It was intended as a rejuvenating force, but though some local gentrification has occurred, the area is still abandoned and isolated. A frightening 1.1-acre outdoor plaza occupied by pigeons and the homeless sits derelict across the street. There was to have been a waterfall and underground access to the centre, but neither facility is functioning. Arriving here as a pedestrian or even by cab is daunting.

Two years behind schedule and $125 million over budget, the project was plagued by problems. Completion took seven years as ideas changed, budgets skyrocketed, and technical problems arose. New York State has a law called Wickes Law which stipulates that plumbing, electrical, structural, mechanical and elevator work all be awarded as separate prime contracts. For the Javits Center there were 62 independent prime construction contracts and new building codes had to be written as there

**I M Pei & Partners 1986**

**I M Pei & Partners 1986**

were no adequate guidelines for such a vast building.

The entire structure is a modified spaceframe and truss system, a light-weight double-layer structure in which steel tubes are connected to spherical nodes. The largest spaceframe in the US, it was constructed of prefabricated components set in tetrahedron patterns. The centre is oriented towards the Empire State Building, sadly turning its back to the water. Along the inner west wall of the internal concourse is a freestanding trapezoidal concrete structure, described by the project architects as a 'building within a building'. This core houses glazed suites from which managers can observe the show floors.

The interior is extraordinary – as dark and ugly as the centre is from the outside, it is light and interesting inside. One can see the entire grey steel structure as well as fantastic views of the city. Piped music and pink marble floor notwithstanding, the concrete benches and columns leave one with the impression that this is just a giant shed constructed with fancy materials.

ADDRESS 655 West 34th Street
CLIENT New York Convention Center Development Corporation, a Subsidiary of New York State Urban Development Corporation
ASSOCIATE ARCHITECTS Lewis, Turner Partnership
STRUCTURAL ENGINEER Weidlinger Associates, Salmon Associates
SIZE 1.6 million square feet (150,000 square metres)
SUBWAY A, C, E to 34th Street/Penn Station
BUS M34, M42
ACCESS lobby open

**I M Pei & Partners 1986**

**I M Pei & Partners 1986**

# Long Island Rail Road Entrance Pavilion

The original Pennsylvania Station, a McKim, Mead & White building from 1910, was one of Manhattan's most regal monuments. The magnificent waiting room was modelled on the Roman Baths of Caracalla and trains rolled into an immense iron and glass shed. The entire 12-acre, four-storey institution was demolished in 1963 and its replacement located 30 feet underground to accommodate Madison Square Garden above.

Penn Station recently underwent a much needed renovation. An integral part of this reworking is a new, strikingly architectonic street-level entrance for the Long Island Rail Road, the only component of the LIRR visible above ground. Penn Station is re-emerging into the world of daylight.

The area in which the new addition is located is alive with constant and hectic movement. Commuters, tourists, shoppers and workers bustle around; Macy's department store and Madison Square Garden add to the pedestrian traffic. Set along a block of single-storey commercial and office buildings, the new entrance is a compelling identifying element for the station. As described by the architects, the project consists of four elements: a brick outer shell, a steel and glass tower, a suspended marquee and an escalator hall. The most aesthetically appealing ingredient is the glass and steel canopy. Extending 21 feet over the sidewalk, this is suspended from thick wire cables that fan down. These are attached to a 107-foot stainless-steel mast. The apex of the mast is a light beacon – a recognisable railroad symbol.

The glass tower, triple height at 92 feet, is completely transparent. Supported structurally by painted steel lace columns and struts, it is very much in keeping with traditional train-station vocabulary. The mullionless curtain walls allow sunlight to illuminate the concourse tunnel by day, while at night artificial light produces a great effect. The glass tower is

**R M Kliment & Frances Halsband Architects 1994**

set into a masonry outer shell that contains cooling towers, stacks and service spaces. Red brick with dark headers in a diagonal pattern, this wall is meant as a protective encasement as well as fulfilling the required programme: to contain climate-control equipment for the underground LIRR concourse.

Also take a look at Maya Lin's *Eclipsed Time*, a sculptural sundial placed in the ceiling of the underground corridor connecting LIRR train platforms and the subway station. An enormous aluminium disc rotates over a 24-hour period obscuring a light source above a fixed glass disk. Conceptually powerful, the installation is unfortunately misplaced and rarely noticed.

ADDRESS Pennsylvania Station
CLIENT Long Island Rail Road
ASSOCIATE ARCHITECTS AND STRUCTURAL ENGINEEER TAMS Consultants
COST $20 million
SIZE 2000 square feet (186 square metres)
SUBWAY 1, 2, 3, 9, A, C, E to 34th Street/Penn Station
BUS M4, M10, M16, M34, Q32
ACCESS open

**R M Kliment & Frances Halsband Architects 1994**

**R M Kliment & Frances Halsband Architects 1994**

# Times Square

The redevelopment (or regression) of Times Square is a large urban 'work in progress' that will have architectural ramifications for the rest of Manhattan. The bow-tied cross-junction where Seventh Avenue, Broadway and West 42nd Street converge is in the process of becoming an outdoor multimedia phenomenon. The most visible pocket of change in Manhattan, these few blocks exemplify the insidious spread of global homogenisation. The passer-by is bombarded with a spellbinding mass of information – enormous billboards and light displays flash advertisements for Calvin Klein, Maxwell, Kodak, various films and up-to-the-minute financial data. A fascinating smorgasbord of consumerist North America, the relentless visual noise is remarkable and lovable. But the driving force behind Times Square's turnaround is less satisfactory.

The New York State Urban Development Corporation, a city and state agency, in collaboration with the New York City Economic Development Corporation, spent more than 14 years and $290 million stamping out Times Square's sex industry. The overriding theme of the rejuvenation programme, titled '42nd Street Now', is sentimentality. As the porn shops and peep shows were cleared, the Disney Corporation claimed a large portion of the site, followed by Madame Tussaud's and MTV. This influx of theme-park masters means that the real centre of Manhattan will now contain an excess of fake urban spaces. Nostalgia-seekers can visit entertainment centres that offer an experience of Manhattan that never was and never will be. Aimed at the less-sophisticated tourist, Times Square is tragically no longer X-rated but a family-style PG.

Though Times Square has been treated as a traditional media centre at a time when the western world is converting to digital media, technological innovation is still at the forefront. The Coca-Cola sign at the centre of the square contains 55 tons of fibre optics. A recent Joe Boxer ad had

**1997**

1997

a ticker wired to the Internet so personal e-mail messages from around the world were seen by the 1.5 million pedestrians who pass through daily – an interesting integration of the private and public realms.

The transformation of Times Square began over a decade ago with the commissioned design of four seemingly identical skyscrapers by Philip Johnson and John Burgee. The scheme was finally scrapped in 1992. Robert A M Stern and graphic designer Tibor Kalman were then retained by the UDC to devise standards for the area, including specifications for the size, scale and positioning of signage. With an effect likened by critics to 'urban taxidermy', these rules are now mandatory for all new edifices.

Some interesting architecture will hopefully emerge, despite the limiting guidelines. Fox & Fowle are designing a new 47-storey skyscraper on Broadway between West 42nd and West 43rd Streets. Hardy Holzman Pfeiffer have done an exemplary job renovating the Victory Theater (allegedly West 42nd Street's first pornographic cinema, now devoted to children's programmes). David Rockwell's dizzying Official All Star Cafe is housed in the Virgin Megastore, designed by BNK Architects and Irvine and Johnston. The most promising project is a hotel and mixed-use complex on West 42nd Street and Seventh Avenue by Florida-based architects Arquitectonica and Disney. Intended as the keystone to the entire redevelopment scheme, this tower will shelter the Disney Vacation Club and is due for completion in the year 2000.

ADDRESS bound by West 42nd and 47th Streets, Broadway and Seventh Avenue
SUBWAY 1, 2, 3, 7, 9, N, R, S to 42nd Street/Times Square
BUS M6, M7, M10, M27, M104
ACCESS open

**Theater and Garment Districts**

**1997**

**The Royalton Hotel**

Chic and silly, this is an entire hotel dedicated to the fashion victim. Do not bother arriving unless you are clad in black and own a mobile phone. Do not be intimidated by the relentlessly beautiful staff.

Once an exclusive bachelor's residence, the neo-Georgian building dates back to 1897. The entire structure was gutted and 171 rooms replaced the original 90. Furniture in the rooms is now built in, inspired by luxury cruise yachts.

The stylish 180-foot-long lobby is part theatrical, part nautical. With its deep blue-carpeted runway and art-deco-style registration desk tucked behind a sumptuous curving mahogany wall, daylight never really reaches this space. Most of the finishes are exquisitely luxurious: rich-hued mahogany, slate, stainless steel, chrome. Waxed-plaster walls offer a backdrop to slipcovered, funky-legged *chaises longues* and high-backed couches. The white slipcovers (the odd violet or peach cover is dotted about) leave the impression that everyone is away on holiday. Or perhaps a repainting job is imminent.

Floral displays mingle with brightly-coloured rope tassels. Mirrors, drapery and many-scaled silver 'Starck drops' abound. The most pretentious space is also the most fun. The champagne bar, a claustrophobic 192-foot circular space, is padded with velvet from top to bottom. The bobbly, azure walls and round stools create a gurgly underwater milieu.

ADDRESS 44 West 44th Street between Fifth and Sixth Avenues
CLIENT 44th Street Hotel Associates
STRUCTURAL ENGINEER Stanley H Goldstein
SUBWAY B, D, F, Q to 42nd Street; 7 to 5th Avenue; 1/9, 2, 3, N, R, S to 42nd Street/Times Square BUS M5, M6, M7, M42, M104
ACCESS open

**Gruzen Samton Steinglass/Philippe Starck 1989**

Theater and Garment Districts

**Theater and Garment Districts**

**Gruzen Samton Steinglass/Philippe Starck 1989**

**Paramount Hotel**

Another of Ian Schrager's trendy hotels, the single-room-occupancy Paramount (completed after The Royalton, page 126) is clever, humorous and less affected. Located in the heart of the theatre district, the rates for its 610 rooms are one-quarter the cost of The Royalton.

The interior layout of the original hotel was kept intact, so each single room is a cosy 12 by 14 feet. The handsome marble and terracotta exterior (designed by Thomas Lamb) was restored to its original 1927 status and a new glass façade placed in the marble arches. An artful floral display – single red roses in symmetrically arranged test tubes covering an entire marble wall – intrigues the passer-by.

Once again, it is the lobby that is the showpiece. Intended as an intimate living room, it has a checkerboard rug littered with mildly tattered Jean-Michel Frank sofas, a Gaudi wooden chair and an operatic aluminium *chaise longue* by Mark Newson. Old-fashioned rotary telephones are strategically placed on side tables to create a homey feel.

A second-floor mezzanine – a chic bar/dining area – is suspended over the open lobby. A spectacular stone and stucco staircase (ideal for a sweeping melodramatic entrance) gives the lobby its visual focal point.

Epigrammatic, ironic touches are everywhere: tilted mirrors with illuminated variable weather forecasts stand in corridors; Vermeer's *The Lacemaker* is silk-screened on the headboard of each room.

ADDRESS 235 West 46th Street
CLIENT Ian Schrager, Philip Pilevsky, Arthur Cohen
STRUCTURAL ENGINEER Stanley H Goldstein, Michael Guilfoyle
SUBWAY 1, 2, 3, 7, 9, N, R, S to 42nd Street/Times Square
BUS M6, M7, M10, M27, M104
ACCESS open

**Haigh Space Architects/Philippe Starck 1992**

**Haigh Space Architects/Philippe Starck 1992**

**D E Shaw & Co**

D E Shaw & Co is a small investment firm, largely computer-driven. Holl sees his design for its 40th-floor offices as 'an analogue to the invisible work done there'.

With a relatively low budget, Holl chose to reinterpret two common – and free – architectural inspirations: space and light. The double-height reception room – an enormous sculptural light box 30 feet high, 21 feet wide and 28 feet long – emanates tranquillity. The northern wall eclipses much of the sensational horizon. This wall and the side walls are double-layer stud and gypsum board; the inner layer has rectilinear cutouts back-painted with a luminous lemon-lime green fluorescent paint that was popular for billboards in the 1950s, and backlit by either sunlight or artificial light. Holl calls this technique 'projected color'. The reflected colour is abstracted and intangible in much the same way as the company's work process is invisible. Elegant details finish the project: the shiny reflective floors are waxed black-vinyl tiles and all closeable doors and skirtings are steel. The conference room has a custom-designed metal table with layered cutouts and translucent glass inserts. Custom-designed light fixtures composed of sandblasted glass cylinders in several different diameters hang above this table.

The interior walls are backlit at night by hidden fluorescent fixtures. Seen from the street, this midtown skyscraper emits a wonderful, mysterious glow from two of its upper floors.

ADDRESS 120 West 45th Street
COST $700,000 SIZE 11,000 square feet (1020 square metres)
SUBWAY B, D, F, Q to 42nd Street; 7 to 5th Avenue; 1/9, 2, 3, N, R, S to 42nd Street/Times Square BUS M5, M6, M7, M42, M104
ACCESS none

**Steven Holl 1992**

**Steven Holl 1992**

# DoubleTree Guest Suites Hotel

This was one of the first projects constructed in compliance with the new signage requirements in Times Square. In 1986 a zoning ordinance was passed that makes large, flashy illuminated signs mandatory on any new structure, the idea being that neon signs are essential to the commercial character of the area. Therefore six floors of this hotel are wrapped with 10,000 square feet of illuminated signage and 120-foot-high curved electronic billboards feature on the façade.

A technically challenging project, the 500-foot, 43-storey skyscraper spans an existing theatre with two 130-foot trusses that sit on four super-columns, two to the east and two to the west. The 57-foot deep composite steel and concrete trusses are connected to 17 smaller trusses that transfer load from the larger bridge trusses to a concrete slab that frames the hotel tower. The tower consists of 38 floors of hotel, public and retail spaces. The five-storey, 1700-seat theatre, design11321ed by Kirchoff & Rose in 1913, was given a new marquee and façade.

ADDRESS 1564–6 Broadway
CLIENT Silverstein Properties
STRUCTURAL ENGINEER DeSimone, Chaplin & Associates
SIZE 460,000 square feet (43,000 square metres)
SUBWAY 1/9 to 50th Street; B, F to 47–50th Street Rockefeller Center; D, E to 7th Ave; N, R to 49th Street
BUS M10, M107
ACCESS lobby open

**Fox & Fowle Architects 1990**

**Fox & Fowle Architects 1990**

**DKNY Penthouse Showroom**

This steel and glass roof pavilion perches like a cockatoo atop a 12-storey building. Crested by an enormous billboard of the DKNY logo, it appears to engage in a skyline dialogue with another giant DKNY billboard blocks away in Times Square. The 28-foot-high vaulted penthouse is like a billboard itself, shouting for recognition. 'It's a head on a body,' states architect Nicholas Goldsmith.

The speedy pace at DKNY – the fashion firm has recently grown to take over the entire building – created the need for versatility. Every element has a double mission: two types of lighting are hidden in suspended troughs underneath the spectacular bowstring trusses of the roof; these troughs also contain display panels of fabric which can be arranged to different effect. A cable-hung retractable stair, inspired by New York's famous fire escapes, can be lowered from a mezzanine to become a catwalk for fashion shows. Sound and video systems can transform the space and recessed bleachers can be pulled out to seat 200. This is a super-duper glam, desperately chic space.

The showroom is accessed by a spiral staircase enclosed in a cylindrical glass shaft. In a reciprocal morphing of interior/exterior, the post-urban rooftop landscape is inside while the visitor has the distinct impression of floating outside over Manhattan's roofscape. Absolutely fabulous!

ADDRESS 240 West 44th Street
CLIENT The Donna Karan Corporation
STRUCTURAL ENGINEER Ross Dalland
COST $4.2 million SIZE 1600 square feet (150 square metres)
SUBWAY 1, 2, 3, 7, 9, N, R, S to 42nd Street/Times Square; A, C, E to 42nd Street BUS M6, M7, M10, M27, M42, M104
ACCESS none

**Theater and Garment Districts**

**FTL Architects 1992**

**Theater and Garment Districts**

**FTL Architects 1992**

# 1585 Broadway

Gwathmey Siegel's first skyscraper has unfriendly proportions and a perturbing skin. Clad in a geometrical pattern of blue-green glass, white patterned glass, mirrored glass, silver aluminium panels and polished stainless steel, the façade is very shiny. An exploration of opacity and reflectivity, the patterning is too busy. The orthogonal grid of Manhattan does not transfer easily to a vertical graphic design.

The building was purchased by the global securities firm Morgan Stanley in the early 1990s and occupied in 1995. As required by zoning rules (see page 122), a supersign was designed (by Gwathmey Siegel). This enormous display consists of two circular 44-foot-high maps with digital multi-timezone clocks featuring, of course, the major financial cities of the world. These maps are surrounded by three 140-foot-long electronic ticker tapes that give 'real-time' information using light-emitting diodes. Decorative mirrorclad fins at street level spell out the building's address.

The building's massing is more successful than its envelope. A stepped base responds to the surrounding shorter buildings of Times Square, leading into a mechanical floor expressed externally as a segmented curve. A rectilinear tower ending in a cutaway top rises from this base.

The interior lobby is very grand. Architectural critic Paul Goldberger writes: 'It ranks among the best public rooms created in this city in the last decade. It is a kind of modernist ballroom.'

ADDRESS 1585 Broadway
ASSOCIATE ARCHITECTS Emery Roth & Sons
STRUCTURAL ENGINEER The Office of Irwin G Cantor
SUBWAY 1/9 to 50th Street; B, F to 47–50th Street Rockefeller Center; D, E to 7th Ave; N, R to 49th Street BUS M10, M107
ACCESS lobby open

**Gwathmey Siegel & Associates Architects 1990**

**Gwathmey Siegel & Associates Architects 1990**

# Worldwide Plaza

The neighbourhood to the west of Times Square, bound by West 30th and West 57th Streets, is known as 'Hell's Kitchen'. Once a hotbed of organised crime and now subject to partial gentrification, its nickname allegedly derives from a conversation between two police officers. While intervening in a summer street scrap, one said to the other, 'It's hot as Hell here.' 'It's cool in Hell. This is Hell's kitchen,' the other replied.

Worldwide Plaza covers a full block, sitting on the site of the old Madison Square Garden. A multi-use complex, composed of a 47-storey office tower, a set of residential buildings and a big public plaza, it was conceived as a transition between the dense commercial sector to the east and the primarily residential Clinton (renamed after the current president) to the west. 'The icon of the skyscraper rather than the highrise' inspired design architect David Childs, who likens his office tower (which sits two blocks west of the Rockefeller Center) to 'the drum major in the Rockefeller band'.

The stone base and brick and clear-windowed vertical shaft above are difficult to reconcile visually as one. Yet the plush circular entry, which brings people in on an internal, elliptical, public pathway that extends the building's perimeter, is a great success and adds punch to the project. The copper-clad pyramidal crown has an inset glass prism which is lit as a beacon at night.

ADDRESS Eighth to Ninth Avenues, West 49th to West 50th Streets
SUBWAY 1/9, C, E to 50th Street
BUS M10, M50, M104
ACCESS entrance, lobby and outdoor plaza open

**Skidmore, Owings & Merrill 1989**

Theater and Garment Districts

**Skidmore, Owings & Merrill 1989**

# The Equitable Center

There is much disagreement among architects and critics about the Equitable. Accused of being bland, blocky and out of proportion, the project's never-ending, almost lickable rose-pink façade is a surprisingly appealing and tactile element. The building's whopping scale is exacerbated by its setback from the road – an extra 10 feet of orange granite pavement that adds to the illusion that this is a grotesquely large stick of striped rock candy. Fourteen-foot setbacks at the 12th, 34th and 50th floors do not detract from the full mass.

The Equitable Life Assurance Society commissioned one of Manhattan's first skyscrapers in 1868. Designed by George B Post, the building at 120 Broadway was destroyed by fire and replaced by a mammoth structure which is still standing today. With no setbacks and an extraordinarily leaden massing, Ernest R Graham's building caused such public outrage that rules on the ratio of site and floor area and stepback regulations were introduced.

The greatest public pleasure at the new site is the art inside. Entering through a great archway (echoed on the exterior apex of the tower) into a five-storey atrium, the visitor is pleasantly overwhelmed by a jolly Lichtenstein, *Mural with Blue Brushstroke*. This delightfully energetic work is balanced by the marvellously calm *Marble Seat Wall with Onyx Lights* by Scott Burton – large glowing chunks of apricot, cream and brown marble resting on the corners of a 40-foot semicircular marble bench.

ADDRESS 787 Seventh Avenue between West 51st and West 52nd Streets
SUBWAY N, R to 49th Street; 1/9 to 50th Street; B, D, F, Q to 47th & 50th
Street Rockefeller Center
BUS M6, M7, M10, M31, M57, M104
ACCESS lobby open

**Edward Larrabee Barnes Associates 1986**

**Edward Larrabee Barnes Associates 1986**

# 750 Seventh Avenue

This surreal sight at the very edge of the Times Square Theater District is a steel tower with a short stubby aerial at its apex that makes it look like a gigantic gadget – perhaps an enormous, upright mobile phone. Local zoning laws required a progressively stepped envelope, and the helical form was intended by Roche to be more dynamic than a series of stacked rectilinear boxes. It does not succeed.

Further exacerbating the project's odd image is its silvery, structurally glazed glass skin. A grid of ceramic-coated glass expressing the horizontal and dark grey reflecting glass expressing the vertical gives 750 Seventh Avenue a strange texture.

ADDRESS 750 Seventh Avenue
STRUCTURAL ENGINEER Weiskopf & Pickworth
COST $45 million
SIZE 530,000 square feet (49,000 square metres)
SUBWAY 1/9 to 50th Street; B, F to 47th–50th Street Rockefeller Center;
D, E to 7th Ave; N, R to 49th Street
BUS M10, M107
ACCESS lobby open

**Kevin Roche John Dinkeloo and Associates 1991**

**Kevin Roche John Dinkeloo and Associates 1991**

**1675 Broadway**

1675 Broadway is a Manhattan office tower designed primarily with real-estate concerns in mind. It was erected at the tail end of the 1980s building boom, when the area surrounding Times Square was considered sweet candy to developers who were offered heady incentives to build here by city planners hoping to decongest midtown.

The tower's intended tenants, corporate law firms, partially informed its envelope, since a plethora of partners required the creation of many corner offices. But the largest design challenge was how to increase the spatial capacity. The developers, Rudin Management, wanted more square footage and larger floor plates than the site could accommodate. The clever solution was the purchase of air rights over the next-door Broadway Theater.

This allowed the 35-storey tower to cantilever 45 feet out over the theatre, vastly increasing the rentable space. The theatre is a landmark building dating from 1924 that could not be touched, and at no point does the cantilever even finger it. Yet the two separate structures – office tower and theatre – blend well visually. The theatre was given a new marquee and façade and the box offices, lobby and lounge were redesigned. Aside from Wednesday matinees, it continued operations, presenting *Les Misérables* throughout the construction period.

Six north–south structural trusses project over the theatre. Four extend through the office tower's elevator core to the south side of the building, countering the weight of the cantilevered side. The supermassive trusses, supported on 32- by 26-inch almost solid steel rectangular columns, weigh up to 200 tons, and some of them support 2000 pounds per foot. As nothing was permitted to rest atop the theatre even temporarily, all the pieces of the trusses were lifted into place by a crane.

Although this structural system is hidden by a curtain wall, the building

**Fox & Fowle Architects 1989**

**Fox & Fowle Architects 1989**

still appears heavy. An elaborate combination of thermal and polished granite does not alleviate the sombre massing. Multiple setbacks and recessed windows add an element of verticality, but sadly the overall effect is unpleasantly monolithic.

ADDRESS 1675 Broadway
CLIENT The Rudin Management Co
STRUCTURAL ENGINEER James Ruderman
SIZE 758,200 square feet (70,440 square metres)
SUBWAY 1/9 to 50th Street; D, E to 7th Avenue; B, F to 47th & 50th Street Rockefeller Center; N, R to 49th Street
BUS M10, M107
ACCESS lobby open

**Fox & Fowle Architects 1989**

**Theater and Garment Districts**

**Fox & Fowle Architects 1989**

**CitySpire**

Dull and ugly, this fast-track mixed-use skyscraper is a blot on the horizon. Chicago-based architect Helmut Jahn has designed a number of skyscrapers in Manhattan, and sadly New York seems to have been the recipient of his least elegant designs. Here 69 monolithic storeys (830 feet high) are topped by a dome vaguely reminiscent of the Moorish dome atop the adjacent City Center Theater. The lower 23 storeys are offices and the upper ones luxury apartments. Two entrances at opposite ends lead through a turretted walkway between West 56th and West 57th Streets. CitySpire's overcomplicated façade with its clumsy massing seems to have been too quickly designed. The tripartite form was partially dictated by zoning regulations, but this is hardly an adequate excuse.

The structural system devised for the project, nicknamed 'shear-wall/open tube' by the structural engineer, is complex. Since it was impossible to devise a fixed-column grid for the irregular configuration of the residential floors, a set of nine separate structural systems was implemented. The central elevator shaft (tube) is connected to the exterior columns through pinwheeling shear walls set between the apartment units. Coupling beams occasionally replace these full-height walls. A multi-diagonal brace creates further reinforcement by rectangular concrete panels staggered from floor to floor. The apex of the building – floors 63 to 69 – is a separate octagonal tower: a culmination of the setbacks that occur throughout the rise of the building.

ADDRESS 150 West 56th Street through to West 57th Street
STRUCTURAL ENGINEER Skidmore, Owings & Merrill
SUBWAY B, N, Q, R to 57th Street; D, E to 7th Avenue
BUS M5, M6, M7, M30, M31, M57
ACCESS lobby open

**Murphy/Jahn 1989**

**Murphy/Jahn 1989**

# Carnegie Hall Tower

On West 57th Street between Sixth and Seventh Avenues stands a curious quartet of buildings. Carnegie Hall Tower, slender and golden, is nearly adjacent to the knife-edge corner of the shiny-black, nouveau Metropolitan Towers, often referred to as the 'Darth Vader building' and the epitome of glitzy 1980s slickness. Sandwiched between them is the diminutive Russian Tea Room – no longer the home of this acclaimed restaurant but still exuding old-world charm. CitySpire (see page 148) – a tacky, fast-track Helmut Jahn addition to the neighbourhood – is visible looming over from West 56th Street. A discussion between the three skyscrapers seems to be in progress: CitySpire is boasting to two very different friends and the Russian Tea Room is struggling to eavesdrop. The forbidding Metropolitan Towers contrasts sharply with Pelli's warm, Cotswold-coloured brick tower.

The second-tallest concrete building in New York City, Carnegie Hall Tower is a commercial venture that uses the air rights of the next-door Carnegie Hall for development. Pelli strove to relate his new building to the culturally iconic, Renaissance revival music hall. The 60-storey tower extends the palette and form of its illustrious neighbour, reinterpreting the music hall's massing, coloration and ornamentation. Pelli likens his position as an architect working within the framework of the city to that of an assistant to a great painter such as Raphael; he sees his role as reinforcing the entire painting, maintaining the coherence of the whole rather than expressing his own creative ego. To Pelli, contextual means mimetic, responsive and appropriate.

The tower is made up of two interlocking slabs of different sizes. A rising tower is set back 31 feet from the street to complement the five-storey Russian Tea Room. The elevations are organised into three parts – two solid corners and a central field – united by wide coloured bands

**Cesar Pelli & Associates 1991**

**Cesar Pelli & Associates 1991**

at six-storey intervals that echo the cornice of the music hall. A dark frieze beneath metal fins tops both the taller tower and the lower building component.

Carnegie Hall Tower is elegantly humble. A cast-in-place concrete structural tube clad in brick, its façade glows with different hues throughout the day. Three complementary colours were used to create the patterns in the central fields – a solution arrived at only after testing thousands of variations.

ADDRESS 152 West 57th Street
CLIENT Rockrose Development Corporation
ARCHITECT OF RECORD Brennan Beer Gorman
STRUCTURAL ENGINEER Robert Rosenwasser Associates
SIZE 530,000 square feet (49,000 square metres)
SUBWAY B, N, Q, R to 57th Street; D, E to 7th Avenue
BUS M6, M7, M31, M57
ACCESS lobby open

**Cesar Pelli & Associates 1991**

**Cesar Pelli & Associates 1991**

# Midtown

# Bryant Park

Urbanistically, New York City develops in small pockets. The addition of a building here or there is not nearly as significant as the rehabilitation, gentrification and redevelopment of the city's public realm, particularly its planned open spaces.

Bryant Park, located in the centre of midtown Manhattan, recently underwent a design overhaul that triggered an enormous change in the surrounding neighbourhood. Coinciding with the restoration of one of Manhattan's beloved architectural gems, the New York Public Library, this project is evidence that excellent design can instigate positive social change.

Notorious as 'Needle Park' during the 1970s and 1980s, Bryant Park was studiously circumvented by all law-abiding New Yorkers. Today, after its redesign, it is estimated that 10,000 people use the park daily. Created in 1846, it was overhauled by parks commissioner Robert Moses in 1934. His neo-classical design, intended to complement the adjacent library, created an enclosed, raised and therefore isolated space.

The major masterplan changes made by Davis, Brody & Associates open up the park through visibility and accessibility. The high stone balustrade and raised walls were lowered or removed and the hedges that wrapped the perimeter of the park were dispensed with. The well-tended lawn has been replanted and Lynden B Miller has created perennial borders 300 feet long by 12 feet deep that are a year-round source of changing beauty. Two hundred plane trees line the gravel paths. Remarkably few of the 200 green wood-and-metal folding chairs provided free to the public ever go missing.

In 1995 kiosks and one of two restaurants within the park designed by Hardy Holzman Pfeiffer Associates were completed. Four dark-green food kiosks stand at the park's corners while two symmetrical sites for

**Davis, Brody & Assocs/Hardy Holzman Pfeiffer Assocs 1992–95**

**Davis, Brody & Assocs/Hardy Holzman Pfeiffer Assocs 1992–95**

restaurant pavilions are located on the west terrace of the library.

The completed restaurant, Bryant Park Grill, has an area of 5250 square feet enclosed in a trelliswork pavilion. Designed as a structure within a structure, the outer envelope is woven aluminium and Paol Lopez wood inset with climbing vines and flowers. This covers an inner skin of glass and steel set with doors that can open the entire pavilion to the elements.

Bryant Park sits above the underground bookstacks for the granite and marble New York Public Library. Even those forward-looking individuals who enjoy only contemporary architecture should have a wander around this grand old edifice. Astor Hall, the main entryway on Fifth Avenue (after you have passed the marvellous stone lions), is one of the rare stone rooms of such a size in the world. Designed by Carrere & Hastings in 1911, this Beaux-Arts delight recently underwent a $20 million multiphase renovation, executed by Davis, Brody & Associates with beautiful care and thoroughness.

ADDRESS West 40th to West 42nd Street
LANDSCAPE ARCHITECTS Lynden B Miller and Hanna/Olin
ASSOCIATE ARCHITECT, LIBRARY RENOVATION Giorgio Cavaglieri for the Gottesman Gallery
STRUCTURAL ENGINEER James Wiesenfeld & Associates
SUBWAY 1/9, 2, 3, N, R, S to 42nd Street Times Square; 7 to 5th Avenue; B, D, F, Q to 42nd Street
BUS M5, M6, M7, M42, M104
ACCESS open

**Midtown**

**Davis, Brody & Assocs/Hardy Holzman Pfeiffer Assocs 1992–95**

**Davis, Brody & Assocs/Hardy Holzman Pfeiffer Assocs 1992–95**

# Permanent Mission of India to the UN

Charles Correa, a leading architect in India, has long been preoccupied with cultural iconography. Many of his buildings make more than a passing reference to ancient Indian spatial ideas; this understated project incorporates these notions very subtly. The colour alone reveals that a fresh viewpoint has been inserted into Manhattan's dense cityscape: the red granite base topped by a canyon red aluminium curtain wall is suggestive of the red sandstone architecture of northern India.

The site is a narrow through block, 42 feet wide on the East 43rd Street side and 24 feet wide on the East 44th Street side. Twenty-eight storeys high, the lower four floors are administrative offices for the Chancery of the Indian government. Above this sit residential quarters for mission employees.

The top of this building is intriguing. Correa has designed a double-height penthouse porch that echoes the Indian *barsati*, used for open-air sleeping. Reading as a wonderful geometrical cutout in rooftop images of the building, sadly it is not very noticeable from ground level. What is readily apparent is the grand, monolithic bronze entryway, reinforcing Correa's reputation as an architect interested not only in the significance of the ancient, but also in the power of authority.

ADDRESS 235 East 43rd Street
ARCHITECT OF RECORD Bond Ryder and Associates
STRUCTURAL ENGINEER Tor, Smollen, Calini & Anastos
SIZE 66,000 square feet (6130 square metres)
SUBWAY 4, 5, 6, 7 or s to Grand Central; 6 to 33rd Street or 51st Street
BUS M1, M2, M3, M4, M42
ACCESS none

**Midtown**

**Charles Correa Architects/Planners 1993**

Midtown

**Charles Correa Architects/Planners 1993**

**The Rainbow Room**

An ear-popping private elevator whizzes one directly to this glittery 65th-floor dinner/dance hall. *Star Trek*-costumed hostesses greet you as you emerge on to the bold checkerboard marble floor. Perhaps one is floating around in outer space on the *Starship Enterprise*? One is actually floating around at the top of Rockefeller Center.

The original Rainbow Room was founded in 1934 as a formal supper club. Reconstructed in a contemporised art-deco style described by architect Hugh Hardy as 'American Modern', its restored spaces are dazzling – grand, vibrant and New York chic. The approach to the renovation was interpretive rather than scientific; Hardy's primary aim was to create a magical, mythical place.

The site contains several venues for private or public entertainment. The two main spaces are the Rainbow Room and the Rainbow Promenade – a restaurant and cocktail lounge with tiered seating for 120 people. One can circle the entire 65th floor and get superlative views of Manhattan. The Rainbow Room is named for its double-height dome, which changes colour regularly above a 32-foot-diameter dance floor that rotates at a rate of 1 foot per minute to give dancers a constantly changing view. The aubergine walls, oak and maple, Austrian crystal, bronze, and geometric patterns make for sparkle everywhere.

ADDRESS 65th Floor, 30 Rockefeller Plaza (Fifth Avenue)
CLIENT Rockefeller Center Management Corporation
STRUCTURAL ENGINEER Edwards & Hjorth
COST $20 million SIZE 50,000 square feet (4600 square metres)
SUBWAY B, D, F, Q to 47th & 50th Street Rockefeller Center; E to 5th Avenue BUS M1, M2, M3, M4, M27, M50, Q32
ACCESS open

**Midtown**

**Hardy Holzman Pfeiffer Associates 1987**

**Hardy Holzman Pfeiffer Associates 1987**

**750 Lexington Avenue**

Helmut Jahn is one of this decade's most prolific architects – perhaps too prolific. Certainly 750 Lexington Avenue is the antithesis of reflective elegance: unwieldy, crude and awkward, it is proof that quality should come before quantity.

A series of geometric volumes, the building consists essentially of a rectangular base interlocked with an octagon that props up a series of graduated cylinders. These nine cylinders start out large and end up quite small with a floating ball balanced on top, producing an effect not unlike that of an elaborate cake. The composition is as static as any 31-storey skyscraper could be, with blue mirrored cladding that denies it any hope of grace.

For a slightly more aesthetically successful Jahn project, see Park Avenue Tower at 65 East 55th Street. Completed in 1987, this is a 36-storey tapered obelisk whose apex is an open, lit, four-sided pyramid that completes the obelisk in traditional fashion. What is disturbing about this structure is not so much its massing and form, as at 750 Lexington Avenue, but the small (6400 square-foot) plaza it is set upon. Sadly this small space interrupts the street wall, creating an awkward sense of site.

ADDRESS 750 Lexington Avenue
CLIENT Cohen Brothers
SIZE 365,000 square feet (34,000 square metres)
SUBWAY 4, 5, 6 to 59th Street; N, R to Lexington Avenue
BUS M31, M57, M101, M102, M103
ACCESS lobby open

**Midtown**

**Murphy/Jahn 1989**

**Murphy/Jahn 1989**

# Linda Dresner Jil Sander

This Park Avenue store is about as sensuous and sleek as a clothing establishment can be. This is rich minimalism that exudes a sensitivity to texture and materials.

Classical proportions, simple spatial configurations and the use of expensive natural materials such as limestone, white marble, black granite, black Macassar ebony and nickel silver create a luxurious environment. Gabellini aims for a sculptural interplay between gravity and a sense of weightlessness, with light considered as part of the architecture. A centrally located giant black box is visible from practically all vantage points, including the exterior. This monolithic, functional object (used for storage) anchors the ethereal interior. A contemporary Rubik's Cube, this box is the basis for a play of black and white tones that resonates throughout the store.

It is a delight to see how the architectural gestures reflect similar qualities to those of the clothing on display: elegance, simplicity of line, and expense.

ADDRESS 484 Park Avenue
COST $600,000
SIZE 4000 square feet (370 square metres)
SUBWAY 4, 5, 6 to 59th Street; N, R to Lexington Avenue
BUS M1, M2, M3, M4, M101, M102, M103, Q32
ACCESS open

Gabellini Associates 1994

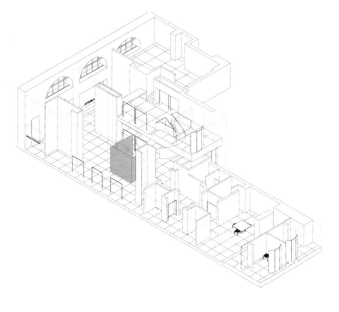

**Midtown**

**Gabellini Associates 1994**

**Museum of Television & Radio**

Designed from the outside in, this is one of Johnson's most contextual projects. Johnson himself describes this white stone temple to television as in the gothic style. Critics have likened its rectilinear bipartite form to a replica of an early radio. I do not think this is what Johnson intended.

The building's programme is to celebrate new media and one can spend hours here looking at recordings, films and videotapes of new and old radio and television programmes.

ADDRESS 23 West 52nd Street
CLIENT William Paley
SUBWAY B, D, F, Q to 47th–50th Rockefeller Center; E to 5th Avenue
BUS M1, M2, M3, M4, M27, M50, Q32
ACCESS open

**John Burgee and Philip Johnson 1990**

Midtown

**John Burgee and Philip Johnson 1990**

# American Craft Museum

A superb staircase – a winding organic sculpture – serves as vertical circulation, organisational focus and marketing tool for this project. Intended as a strike against post-modernism, the simple white stairs snake sensuously through the front of the museum, slicing a vertical pathway across the entire space. Visible from the street through the building's expansive glass curtain wall, they exert a magical pull, drawing in the passer-by; from the inside they are equally successful, giving a marvellous view of the tree-lined street through the same curtain wall as well as affording stunning perspectives of the work within. The staircase is craftwork worthy of its permanent exhibition, unfolded through experimentation on site rather than at the drawing board: a freehand outline was traced on site and lengths of the parapet roughed out; after refinements at a wood-carver's shop, the smoothing and finishes were also done *in situ*.

The American Craft Council's museum occupies four storeys of a pink granite 35-storey tower. The basement floor has been excavated so a mezzanine could be placed halfway below grade, cleverly bypassing city zoning regulations governing floor-area ratios. In the lower stairwells the serpentine steps wrap into niches perfect for intimate displays.

Flexibility was an important factor. Innovative wooden ceiling grids inset with tracks and rollers allow the reorganisation of hanging displays. Lighting fixtures are hidden above these modules. The maple floors reflect this ceiling grid, creating a cohesive environment.

ADDRESS 44 West 53rd Street
STRUCTURAL ENGINEER Office of Irwin G Cantor
SUBWAY B, D, F, Q to 47th & 50th Street Rockefeller Center; E to 5th Avenue BUS M1, M2, M3, M4, M27, M50, Q32
ACCESS open

**Midtown**

**Fox & Fowle Architects 1987**

Midtown

**Fox & Fowle Architects 1987**

**Sony Building**

'A building in New York needs a good top and a good bottom,' said Philip Johnson in a recent discussion with me about his work in Manhattan. Sitting in Johnson's office in the Lipstick Building, which he designed in 1986 (see page 190), the view of the top of the former AT&T Building (now the Sony Building) gave weight to this statement. The Sony Building certainly possesses one of the most famous tops and bottoms in New York. Each element of the pink granite-clad tripartite composition – base, centre and apex – is monumental. The six-storey loggia has a 65-foot-high cross-vaulted arch; the massive crowning pediment instantly identifies the building. Initially considered controversial, this much marketed and hyped edifice is now not only an icon of midtown Manhattan but a historic symbol of the birth of American post-modern classicism.

Johnson's buildings always seem to receive nicknames and this one is no exception. It is referred to affectionately as the 'Chippendale building' because of its top: a mammoth pediment drilled into by an orbiculum that resembles the ornamentation found on 17th-century chairs designed by Thomas Chippendale. The project has been harshly criticised as pompous, corporate and impudent. I am quite fond of the top: it is an elegant exploration of solid and void and its easy-recognition factor lends hospitality to Manhattan's hectic skyline.

The commissioning clients AT&T moved out of the premises in the early 1990s and the building was sold to the Japanese-owned Sony Corporation. Gwathmey Siegel & Associates was hired to reconfigure the space to accommodate 1600 employees instead of AT&T's 600. The entire interior was gutted and reworked. Sony desired a considerably less formal image, and wanted the base of the building to be more user friendly. The new architects negotiated with the city to exchange a floor-area bonus for the reconfiguration of the street-level public area.

**Philip Johnson/John Burgee 1984; Gwathmey Siegel & Assocs 1994**

Midtown

**Philip Johnson/John Burgee 1984; Gwathmey Siegel & Assocs 1994**

The 60-foot neo-Renaissance arcades that flank the north and south sides of the original building were enclosed with aluminium-framed bay windows and air conditioned, creating a galleria and retail spaces. A news-stand, commissary, ticket booth and the Sony Wonder Museum were installed. Black glass was fitted into arched recesses, dividing the massing of the existing walls, but the ceiling height was retained. The narrow outdoor arcades along East 55th and 56th Streets were kept intact as they provide a much needed covered passageway during the colder months.

ADDRESS 550 Madison Avenue
STRUCTURAL ENGINEER Thornton Thomasetti
SIZE 200,000 square feet (18,600 square metres)
SUBWAY B, Q to 57th Street; E, F, N, R to 5th Avenue
BUS M1, M2, M3, M4, M31, M57
ACCESS arcade open

**Philip Johnson/John Burgee 1984; Gwathmey Siegel & Associates 1994**

**Philip Johnson/John Burgee 1984; Gwathmey Siegel & Associates 1994**

**Trump Tower**

An ostentatious advertisement for conspicuous consumption and mega-lomaniacal immortalisation of all that Ivana and Donald Trump stood for at the frozen golden moment of its construction, this 68-storey skyscraper is an indisputable icon of the 1980s. The building's overblown, *Dynasty*-style environment still inspires innumerable tourists to video their shopping experiences.

The commercial interior is a seductive magical kingdom, shimmering with relentlessly glamorous glitz. Pink mirrorglass, polished bronze trim and the capital letter T abound. The double-height entryway leads through a 30-foot-wide treelined arcade to a six-storey atrium – a skylit space surrounded by shops, boutiques and speciality stores. The extravagant rose, peach and orange Italian marble back wall enclosing the six balconied floors is covered by an illuminated waterfall that cascades down into a garden concourse one level below the street.

The warmth of the interior of this temple to excess was not successfully translated to the exterior. It is the tallest concrete building in New York (664 feet high), with its façade a series of black sawtoothed vertical setbacks. Above the atrium are 13 floors of offices and above that 263 luxury condominium apartments: Steven Spielberg, Michael Jackson, Sophia Loren, the Sultan of Brunei and Sir Andrew Lloyd Webber allegedly keep apartments here.

ADDRESS 725 Fifth Avenue
SUBWAY B, Q to 57th Street; E, F, N, R to 5th Avenue
BUS M1, M2, M3, M4, M31, M57
ACCESS atrium and shopping floors open

**Midtown**

**Der Scutt/Swanke Hayden Connell Architects 1983**

**Der Scutt/Swanke Hayden Connell Architects 1983**

# OMO Norma Kamali

Gold lamé banners ripple in the Manhattan breeze on the cubist façade of this superbly designed shop. The chances of spotting a celebrity shopper are high: Broadway *diva* Patti Lupone was trying on lavender jackets in the stone-coloured interior landscape when I was last there.

Contemporary romanesque, the store is a combination of Carlo Scarpa, drama and drop-dead glamour. In the front window zinc statues of the Four Seasons clothed in classical gowns pose coyly on textured cement. The townhouse interior was completely gutted and refaced to meet the client's request for strong monolithic forms enclosing a sequence of intimate spaces that would create a continuous sense of discovery. Each price range of clothing occupies a separate area of the multi-level tiers, with the roundabout circulation past artfully positioned classical busts suggestive of a walk through ancient ruins.

The raw materials – textured stucco walls and hand-trowelled cement-plaster floors – provide an understated background for the sensuous clothing on display, which is meant to be read as a series of timeless arte-facts. Different materials demarcate different spaces: a tile floor mimicking a swimming pool defines the bathing-suit department; evening clothes are framed by a fanciful entryway atop slate steps. The display counters and lighting fixtures were handcrafted.

ADDRESS 11 West 56th Street
ASSOCIATE ARCHITECTS Peter Michael Marino Architects
STRUCTURAL ENGINEER Robert Silman Associates
SIZE 10,000 square feet (930 square metres)
SUBWAY B, Q to 57th Street; E, F, N, R to 5th Avenue
BUS M1, M2, M3, M4, M5, M6, M7, M31, M57
ACCESS open

**Rothzeid Kaiserman Thomson & Bee 1984**

Midtown

**Rothzeid Kaiserman Thomson & Bee 1984**

# Henri Bendel

Posh, posh, posh! This sumptuous women's speciality store is the epitome of understated luxury. With a pedigree that includes downtown Barneys – the temple of 1980s Manhattan pretension on Seventh Avenue and West 17th Street – as well as the renovation of Fenwicks in London's Bond Street, the architects have created a new five-storey building that echoes the scale and architectural elegance of its restored landmark neighbours, the Rizzoli and Coty buildings. The tripartite façade of toasty limestone, white granite and wood casement windows feels very Frenchified, a nod to the exquisite three-storey etched-glass window of twisting vines and poppies that dominates the Coty façade, the only known example of architectural glass by French master René Lalique. Each of the three buildings sports a polished bronze and steel storefront.

One steps through heavy brass doors into a grand, four-storey French limestone and marble central atrium (inspired by 1920s Parisian *maisons de couture*) with two elliptical staircases surrounded by glorious galleries of speciality boutiques. A skylit oculus acts as a reflective kaleidoscope. The juxtaposition of the funky, colourful displays and the impeccably proper building's beiges, blacks and transparencies exaggerates the pricey feel. It is possible to get quite close to the Lalique window while mingling with Chanel-clad mannequins.

ADDRESS 712 Fifth Avenue and 56th Street
STRUCTURAL ENGINEER Weiskopf & Pickworth
SIZE 80,000 square feet (7400 square metres)
SUBWAY B, Q to 57th Street; E, F, N, R to 5th Avenue
BUS M1, M2, M3, M4, M5, M31, M57, Q32
ACCESS open

**Midtown**

**Beyer Blinder Belle 1991**

**Beyer Blinder Belle 1991**

Midtown

**Four Seasons Hotel**

'Designed to continue the grand condition of a former time when going to a hotel was an occasion, The Four Seasons' emphasis is not on workaday efficiency ... but on celebrating the luxury hotel experience.' So reads the publicity for this enormous stageset hotel. The exterior of this behemoth is vulgar, overscaled and overgrand, but the excruciating main façade is redeemed by a dignified interior.

The tallest hotel in Manhattan, the Four Seasons stands 51 storeys above ground (682 feet high). Its 6-acre site is a through-block assemblage of three adjacent parcels of land located in two separate districts. Zoning transfers were not approved, so the two street façades had to oblige two separate sets of ordinances.

The pavement outside the main East 57th Street entrance has a radial pattern echoing the fussy, cantilevered steel and glass petal entrance canopy. The massing is a series of setbacks demarcated by 12-foot lanterns at each setback. Intricate windows and sculptural stone sills attempt to capture a residential feel that differentiates the hotel from the nearby office towers.

The architectural design process was from the inside out. A preliminary decision about the size and shape of the guest rooms (600 square feet) was arrived at. These were then assembled into floorplates which were stacked as building blocks to form an incremental tower within the available zoning envelope. Perhaps this is why the inside is so successful and the outside a disaster.

The grand foyer is a tall cube of space, approximately 32 feet square by 37 feet high. Reached through a 28-foot-wide entrance, it is the focal point of a carefully thought-out promenade through the heroic dimensions of superb urban theatre. This spectacular lobby/court has terraced salon-style lounges on either side.

**Pei Cobb Freed & Partners 1993**

Midtown

**Pei Cobb Freed & Partners 1993**

Taking lunch at the hotel is enormously calming: the uniform materials palette of nickel silver, oxidised bronze and Danish beechwood set against the honey-coloured walls of Magny de Louvre limestone (the same as on the exterior) and vast geometric space create a tranquillity much appreciated on this frenzied shopping street.

ADDRESS 57 East 57th Street
ASSOCIATE ARCHITECT Frank Williams Associates
STRUCTURAL ENGINEER Robert Rosenwasser Associates
CLIENT 57-57th Associates
SIZE 532,227 square feet (49,446 square metres)
SUBWAY 4, 5, 6 to 59th Street; E, F, N, R to Lexington Avenue
BUS M1, M2, M3, M4, M31, M57
ACCESS lobby and restaurants open

Midtown

**Pei Cobb Freed & Partners 1993**

**Pei Cobb Freed & Partners 1993**

**135 East 57th Street**

It would be virtually impossible not to notice this building. A concave 31-storey tower has been set back from the sidewalk to space for a massive three-storey tempietto.

The tower itself has been divided into two distinct masses. A flat street-wall façade faces 57th Street and the corner façade curves away from the sidewalk to create a circular plaza. One becomes extremely aware that this is a corner.

Zoning requirements and the programme dictated the massing. There are separate entries for the many functions: an antiques centre, an office block and a series of two-storey townhouses. Place des Antiquaires, an important centre of New York's antiques trade, is represented by the tempietto. The marble fountains, grey granite paving and greenery seem odd, if refreshing, at this overcrowded intersection. The tower's main entrance is located behind the plaza, on a direct axis with the tempietto. Is it the vast expanse of empty space, the sheer scale of the building or the presence of a marble garden folly in the middle of the city that is so disconcerting?

ADDRESS 135 East 57th Street
CLIENT Madison Equities
SIZE 429,000 square feet (39,900 square metres)
SUBWAY 4, 5, 6 to 59th Street; E, F, N, R to Lexington Avenue
BUS M1, M2, M3, M4, M31, M57
ACCESS lobby open

**Midtown**

**Kohn Pedersen Fox Associates 1988**

Kohn Pedersen Fox Associates 1988

# Monkey Bar

An elegant bar stool in the shape of a martini olive sounds like a contradiction in terms. Nevertheless, David Rockwell has achieved just that – charming and sophisticated giant cocktail olives (complete with pimento stuffing) on which to plant one's bottom.

Named for the 'monkey business' that happens at watering holes universally, the original Monkey Bar opened in 1936. Recently redesigned by Rockwell, the bar has now been joined by an adjacent restaurant.

The only remaining element from the original is the fantastic murals by Charlie Vella. These images of anthropomorphic monkeys splattered across a faded ochre backdrop set the space's cultivated tone. The monkey motif is everywhere – cast monkeys swing across the lighting fixtures – yet the bar is surprisingly ungimmicky in comparison with other of Rockwell's themed projects.

The palette of cobalt blue, yellow and russet is a lush combination. The bar is swank, suave and debonair, right down to the materials and finishes: leather, velvet, cast-bronze railings and bamboo-look crown mouldings. Don't miss the wonderful stylised skyscraper screens in the corners of the dining room.

ADDRESS Hotel Elysee, 60 East 54th Street
SIZE 3155 square feet (293 square metres)
SUBWAY 6 to 51st Street; E, F to 5th Avenue
BUS M1, M2, M3, M4, M31, M57, M101, M102, M103
ACCESS open

**Midtown**

**Rockwell Group 1994**

**Rockwell Group 1994**

# 885 Third Avenue (Lipstick Building)

Philip Johnson is remarkable among the architectural community for his close relationships with several developers. But unlike many of the jaded architects who work with developers, artful design has always been of great importance to Johnson and the outward appearance of his buildings has always been given a great deal of thought. Manhattan is dotted with several of his wonderful works. Hailed as the forefather of American post-modernism, most of his output should be classified as eclectic. Romantic, sculptural and dynamic, his architecture has made an interesting impact on the Manhattan skyline.

According to Johnson, the developers for this project were not convinced that the address had the Manhattan marketing requisite of 'location, location, location', so part of his brief was to design as beautiful a form as possible. The result is a 36-storey brown granite and glass ellipse created by three overlapping tiers. Nicknamed the Lipstick Building because of its resemblance to a posh cosmetics case, the entire structure rests on thin twinset columns that circle the base, allowing the passer-by to walk underneath the seductive curved shape.

ADDRESS 885 Third Avenue
CLIENT Gerald D Hines
SUBWAY B, D, F, Q to 47th–50th Rockefeller Center; E to 5th Avenue
BUS M1, M2, M3, M4, M27, M50, Q32
ACCESS lobby and ground-floor restaurant open

**Midtown**

**John Burgee and Philip Johnson 1986**

SALAD
BAR

HOT
FOOD

?35-9176

CHARLTON'S

ART GALLERY

# Bumble + Bumble

Industrial suction cups hold a futuristic robotic device to the window of this hip hair salon. Extending metal limbs in all directions, this strange creature displays photographs, video monitors and metal *objets d'art*. Behind it stands the galvanised-metal and wood reception box.

Ross Anderson: 'The salon places you on display while you simultaneously view others. Transparency, translucency, opacity: spaces and objects are revealed through materials and shapes, creating anticipation. With unexpected combinations of architectural elements and reiterated materials, connections are formed that give the salon a coherence. Clients participating in their own transformation also participate in ours.'

It is very agreeable to sit in this large blue space and admire the fine architectural details: cutting stations fabricated from poured-concrete counters; lights and mirrors supported by aluminium brackets; fibreglass panels mounted over steel frames. The colour stations upstairs are designed like steamer trunks: the maple plywood and blackened steel frames fold up and roll away to free the space for photo shoots and seminars. When unlocked, they plug into a power grid in the stained plywood floor which was inspired by a drawing by Brice Marden. The drawing is meant to be added to over time by the goops dropped by the colourists.

Italian architects Dario Caimi and Franco Asnaghi's furniture showroom for Cassina across the street is also worth a look.

ADDRESS 146 East 56th Street
STRUCTURAL ENGINEER Gilsanz Murray Steficek
COST $1.68 million SIZE 16,800 square feet (1560 square metres)
SUBWAY 4, 5, 6 to 59th Street; N, R to Lexington Avenue
BUS M31, M57, M101, M102, M103
ACCESS by appointment only

**Anderson/Schwartz Architects 1996**

**Anderson/Schwartz Architects 1996**

**Calvin Klein**

Opening to huge publicity, this minimalist venue helped kick start an invasion of designer flagship boutiques in the Madison Avenue neighbourhood (East 51st Street to East 72nd Street). Ralph Lauren's enormous headquarters at the Rhinelander Mansion on Madison Avenue and 72nd Street probably initiated the trend, but Klein's showcase followed soon after. Newcomers in the last year include Moschino, Valentino, Prada, Etro and two Armani shops. Fifth Avenue also has several new million-dollar spaces housing Versace, Ferragamo, Piaget and Revilion while 57th Street now has a weird mix of low- and high-end shops – new here are Chanel, Niketown and Warner Brothers.

Functioning both as global advertising tools and tourist attractions, these flagship stores are paragons of excess. The Chanel building, a tall narrow grey-granite and steel tower designed by Platt Byard Dovell, is an elegant classical oasis amid the sad suburban kitsch of Warner, Disney and Niketown. Chanel will eventually be joined by a tower (currently under construction) designed by French architect Christian de Portzamparc for LVMH (Louis Vuitton–Moët Hennessy). This exciting project is certain to be a vast improvement on Armani's flagship store at Madison Avenue and East 65th Street by the designer of the Vuitton and Valentino interiors, Peter Marino (see page 178). This four-storey French limestone concoction is just about acceptable from afar but reveals itself as appalling on closer inspection; a shockingly complex internal circulation system combined with poor finishes contrasts sharply with Armani's impeccably designed clothes.

Calvin Klein, designed by British minimalist John Pawson, is clean and streamlined. Minimalism has only recently arrived in commercial Manhattan and Americans tend to imbue this more British concept with an eclecticism that dilutes the austere, serene effect. Pawson's prototypical

**John Pawson 1995**

**John Pawson 1995**

space is no exception. The site was once a bank and the exterior ionic pilasters were retained. Enormous vertical panes of glass (34 feet high) framed with limestone were slid between these columns.

The multi-level interior is anchored around the concept of white, used in several shades. An intentionally limited materials palette consists of matte Yorkshire sandstone, stainless steel and ebony-stained walnut. Three floors (that finish 1 foot short of the enormous windows) with an added mezzanine and basement contain the simply designed necessities: narrow rectangular mirrors, stainless-steel hanging rods, fitting rooms. The basement floor, stocked with home furnishings, is overwhelmed by reproductions/re-editions of Donald Judd tables, benches and beds. These austere, perfectly proportioned art pieces call attention to Pawson's cramped circulation, shabby finishes and distorted sense of scale.

ADDRESS 654 Madison Avenue
STRUCTURAL ENGINEER De Nardis Associates
SUBWAY 4, 5, 6 to 59th Street; N, R to Lexington Avenue
BUS M31, M57, M102, M103
ACCESS open

**John Pawson 1995**

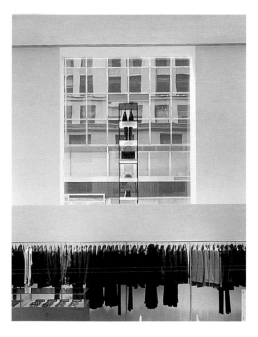

**John Pawson 1995**

Midtown

# Upper East Side and Roosevelt Island

**Metropolitan Museum of Art**

A long-term project: masterplanning for the museum's expansion began in 1967 and construction continued throughout the early 1990s.

The museum, which celebrated its 125th anniversary in 1995, is a magnificent combination of Victorian gothic, Beaux-Arts and modernism. The major players were Calvert Vaux and Jacob Wrey Mould; Richard Morris Hunt; McKim, Mead & White; and Kevin Roche John Dinkeloo and Associates. Christened 'the palace in the park', it was not until 1903 that the entrance façade was oriented by Hunt to Fifth Avenue. McKim, Mead & White added to this façade and turned the corner on the north and south sides. Kevin Roche felt that the newest additions should not be so formal: 'an architecture more like the kind of building one would expect to find in a park, like a greenhouse in a botanical garden'.

The result is archaeological: a building composed of strata of overlapping architectures. For instance, the most visible aspect of the original Vaux and Wrey Mould Victorian gothic structure is now the east wall of Roche Dinkeloo's Robert Lehman Wing, while the grand staircase leading to the stately Fifth Avenue entrance – added by Roche Dinkeloo in 1970 – hides Hunt's original rusticated base and so transforms the overall composition.

The need for the expansion – the most extensive reconstruction of any museum in the US – was precipitated by the receipt of the Temple of Dendur (1st century BC) from the United Arab Republic in 1965 and the forthcoming bicentennial celebrated by America in 1976. The initial phase was the redesign of the west elevation including the front plaza and entry into the restored great hall. The entry axis was then reinforced by the addition of the skylit Lehman Pavilion on the west façade. The Robert Lehman Wing (1975), the Temple of Dendur in the Sackler Wing (1978),

**Kevin Roche John Dinkeloo and Associates 1967–90**

the new American Wing (1980) and the Michael C Rockefeller Wing (1982) all followed.

The four newest additions are the Lila Acheson Wallace Wing completed in 1987, the Iris and B Gerald Cantor Roof Garden completed in 1987, the Tisch Galleries completed in 1988, and the Henry R Kravis Wing and Carroll and Milton Petrie European Sculpture Court completed in 1990.

ADDRESS Fifth Avenue at East 82nd Street
STRUCTURAL ENGINEER Severud Associates
COST $190 million
SIZE 1.3 million square
feet (120,000 square metres)
SUBWAY 4, 5, 6 to 86th Street
BUS M1, M2, M3, M4, M86
ACCESS open

**Kevin Roche John Dinkeloo and Associates 1967–90**

**Kevin Roche John Dinkeloo and Associates 1967–90**

# Guggenheim Museum Addition

Frank Lloyd Wright's Guggenheim Museum is perhaps the last building erected in Manhattan to have pioneered a new typology. This circular concrete structure, designed around a seven-storey spiral ramp, introduced fresh ideas about organising space and viewing art. Opened to the public in 1959, it immediately became an icon. Wright himself christened the Guggenheim his 'Temple in the Park'.

Many architects and critics felt that the building as it stood was a work of art: one would not embellish a painting by van Gogh, so why add to the Guggenheim? Yet buildings are not art and the programmatic life of a building must include the capacity to reconfigure, renovate and expand. Charles Gwathmey has stated in a written response to his critics (published in *Architectural Record*, October 1992) that: 'Architecture is not static, nor is its perception. We believe in the idea of the addition as much as in its realisation: a modern, referential intervention, which supports the formal intentions and precedents of the original building, while extending its ideal and its reality.'

Some critics argue that Gwathmey Siegel took the easy way out, following plans drawn up by Wright in 1949 to create a building truer to Wright than the freestanding concrete spiral that was constructed. Others have derided the new configuration as resembling a toilet bowl and tank.

The two-year renovation and expansion created a new ten-storey annex to the east of the original edifice. Clad with a mesh-patterned limestone, the rectilinear extension, an understated textured box, integrates beautifully with the rotunda and provides the perfect backdrop for the dramatic spiral. What used to be a freestanding sculptural object now resembles a three-dimensional abstraction of a cubist painting, its volume part of a greater composition.

**Gwathmey Siegel & Associates Architects 1992**

**Gwathmey Siegel & Associates Architects 1992**

The new tower houses four stacked viewing galleries, two upper floors of offices and a mechanical floor. Ten thousand square feet of auxiliary space was added beneath the Fifth Avenue sidewalk. The interior junctions where new meets old are wonderfully executed. The roof of the rotunda interrupts the newer areas, unexpected bits of copper roof and cast stone jutting into the white exhibition space.

Several changes were made to the original structure. The top of the sloping spiral, closed off by a previous director, was reopened as usable gallery space. New thermal skylights were installed, creating a wonderful wash of light over the entire ramp (the original skylight had not been cleaned since 1959). The existing smaller rotunda was reprogrammed to become a gift shop on the lower floor with exhibition space above. A cafeteria planned according to a Wright design was positioned at the back of the ground floor and a 900-square-foot sculpture terrace has been added at the fifth floor. This small but wonderful space provides the opportunity for close inspection of the exterior junction of new and old as well as a spectacular view over Central Park.

ADDRESS Fifth Avenue at East 89th Street
STRUCTURAL ENGINEER Severud Associates
SIZE 135,000 square feet (12,500 square metres)
SUBWAY 4, 5, 6 to 86th Street
BUS M1, M2, M3, M4, M86
ACCESS open

**Gwathmey Siegel & Associates Architects 1992**

**Upper East Side and Roosevelt Island**

**Gwathmey Siegel & Associates Architects 1992**

# Jewish Museum Addition

The Jewish Museum originally occupied two linked buildings on Fifth Avenue: the historic landmark 1908 Warburg Mansion and the 1962 List Building and Courtyard. Designed in the same style and to the same height as C P H Gilbert's Beaux-Arts mansion, the 1993 addition is almost imperceptible. It is as if by magic the Warburg had been pulled, stretched and tweaked.

The gallery space has been doubled and classrooms and a 232-seat auditorium added. Fragments of the existing building are incorporated into the interior and dormers and bits of cornice relocated on the exterior. This was a controversial project and many, including myself, feel that Kevin Roche missed an opportunity to effect a bold, meritorious architectural gesture. Roche explains his design as fulfilling the wishes of his clients and demonstrative of one of the many roles an architect must assume: 'I did not allow myself an ego-trip.'

Roche is also the architect for A Living Memorial to the Holocaust, The Museum of Jewish Heritage. Located on a narrow triangular site in Battery Park City, this 20,700-square-foot, two-storey six-sided (as a reminder of the 6 million who died and reference to the six-pointed Star of David) granite building appears austere. The upper floor has large windows that overlook the bay and bring into view the Statue of Liberty. The louvered roof allows further light to filter in.

ADDRESS 1109 Fifth Avenue
STRUCTURAL ENGINEER Severud Associates
COST $21 million SIZE 29,700 square feet (2,760 square metres)
SUBWAY 6 to 96th Street
BUS M1, M2, M3, M4, M96
ACCESS open

**Kevin Roche John Dinkeloo and Associates 1993**

**Kevin Roche John Dinkeloo and Associates 1993**

# Asphalt Green Recreational Complex

Here stands a giant concrete parabola. Designed by Ely Jacques Kahn and Robert Allan Jacobs in the 1940s, the structure – a former asphalt-manufacturing plant – is a parabolic arched steel frame composed of four prefabricated ribs, 90 feet high and 22 feet apart, cased in a series of concrete panels joined together as continuous barrel vaults. Influenced by French dirigible hangars (Jacobs worked for Le Corbusier in the 1930s) as well as the machinery required to mix asphalt, the plant was in operation until 1968 and manufactured much of the asphalt used to fill New York's potholes.

In 1982 Pasanella + Klein and Hellmuth, Obata & Kassabaum collaborated to convert the defunct plant into a public/private recreational space, the George and Annette Murphy Center. Sitting in the northern corner of this narrow triangular site is the complex's serpentine showpiece. A five-storey red-brick façade with lime-green and cerulean-blue trim undulates seductively: an exterior suggestive of the parabola, the riverside and the indoor Natatorium it houses. The internal composition and external footprint were determined by the possession of the only Olympic-size pool in Manhattan.

This non-profit-making, primarily privately funded complex hopes to produce an Olympic gold medallist – hence the 4- by 12-foot underwater observation window that enables coaches to analyse technique. There is a sliding scale of fees for individuals with limited incomes.

ADDRESS 1750 York Avenue
STRUCTURAL ENGINEER Goldreich, Page & Thropp
COST $24 million SIZE 74,250 square feet (6,898 square metres)
SUBWAY 4, 5 to 86th Street; 6 to 96th Street BUS M31, M86
ACCESS lobby open; facilities can be used for a daily fee

**Richard Dattner Architect 1993**

**Richard Dattner Architect 1993**

**Islamic Cultural Center**

A traditional mosque and religious gathering place bizarrely built out of familiar New York materials: granite, marble, glass.

Sponsored by the Islamic nations of the UN, the centre serves the local community as well as visiting diplomats. Attendance on an average Friday night can number over 1000. A school and library are currently being constructed on an adjacent plot to supplement the existing classrooms and administrative offices.

The cubic building – composed of repeated square units – is topped by a steel, glass and concrete dome. The interior has a 90-foot clear-span column-free worship hall rotated to face Mecca. All flat ornament is also derived from square patterns: floating granite panels, framed by glass strips, are supported by a hidden grid of tubular steel.

The dramatic entryway is 15 feet high and composed of layered, geometrically patterned green glass (green is associated with paradise in Islam). The interior sports a diminutive women's gallery – it is a complaint among regulars that not enough space was allocated to women worshippers – facing the *mihrab* (prayer wall) and structurally suspended from the four trusses that support the copper-clad dome. A sculptural gesture – a large circle of steel wire-hung lamps meant to symbolise oil lamps – lights up the carpeted worship hall.

Shoes must be removed and women wear the hooded caftans provided.

ADDRESS 1711 Third Avenue
ARCHITECTS FOR MINARET Swanke Hayden Connell Architects
STRUCTURAL ENGINEER Richard Rowe
COST $17 million SIZE 21,000 square feet (1,950 square metres)
SUBWAY 6 to 96th Street BUS M96, M101, M102, M103
ACCESS open

**Skidmore, Owings & Merrill 1991**

**Skidmore, Owings & Merrill 1991**

# Guggenheim Pavilion, Mount Sinai Medical Center

This is a vast project, covering a full square block facing Central Park.

The 11-storey façade is neutral brick and limestone. A barely perceptible thread of lavender, buff and grey hand-laid bricks reduces the enormous mass. Classical limestone details and trim and the bronze borders of the repeated square windows soften the institutional character. The building blends in well with its surroundings and could aptly be described as pleasant.

Three towers rise from a rectangular base. Triangular cuts in these towers create two large tree-filled courtyards. These public atriums plus a third skylit plaza were the organising elements. The plaza serves as circulation, connecting some two-thirds of the centre at ground-floor level. The complex programme called for 625 patient beds, 22 new operating rooms, a new emergency room, rehabilitation and nuclear medicine, admissions, a cafeteria, a conference centre and auditorium, a kitchen, administrative offices, a chapel and a synagogue.

ADDRESS Fifth to Madison Avenues, East 98th to 102nd Streets
ASSOCIATE ARCHITECT Ellerbe Architects & Engineers
STRUCTURAL ENGINEER Weiskopf & Pickworth
COST $218 million
SIZE 900,707 square feet (83,678 square metres)
SUBWAY 6 to 103rd Street
BUS M1, M2, M3, M4, M96
ACCESS lobby open

**Pei Cobb Freed & Partners 1992**

Upper East Side and Roosevelt Island

**Pei Cobb Freed & Partners 1992**

**PS 217**

Three hundred yards across the East Channel of the East River is a 2-mile-long island. Once known as Welfare Island, it was rechristened Roosevelt Island in 1971. Advertised then as the 'New Town in Town' by New York State Urban Development Corporation, it is car free, accessed by tramway, subway or bus.

Once on this grim island, it is difficult to determine what city, state, country or continent one is in. Highly residential (3000 units to date), it has government-subsidised housing next door to the homes of wealthy UN diplomats. Populated with both abandoned and functioning hospitals, with Octagon Tower, the central core of the former New York City Lunatic Asylum, morbidly crumbling at one end, it is as if disembodied ghouls echo around every corner.

Shining jubilantly amid this sour urban experiment is PS 217, a decidedly deconstructivist public school. Its architecture is assertive and gallant, particularly in light of its difficult surroundings. Grids within grids organise four primary elements around a courtyard. Classrooms occupy a narrow four-storey block with a rotated two-storey cube sitting slightly askew inside. The modular grid is repeated in various scales and materials throughout: as a concrete sunshade, glass fenestration and a cantilevered metal frame. Formal geometry and tough urban materials are enlivened by sunny primary colours. The edifice dextrously addresses its waterfront site while simultaneously creating a private enclave for the 850 kindergarten-to-eighth-grade students who attend.

ADDRESS 645 Main Street, Roosevelt Island
COST $2.2 million SIZE 108,000 square feet (10,030 square metres)
SUBWAY B, Q to Roosevelt Island BUS Q102
ACCESS none

**Michael Fieldman & Partners 1992**

**Michael Fieldman & Partners 1992**

# Central Park

# Wollman Memorial Rink

Any look at architecture in New York City cannot deal simply with individual projects but must become something of an urban study. Manhattan and its five boroughs cover a vast territory and pockets of development in conjunction with particular buildings can have enormous ramifications.

One of the areas that has undergone considerable change within the last decade is Central Park. A design *parti* for Manhattan, America's first urban park is both a formal organisational element in New York's master-plan and a wonderful, well-used outdoor space. A work of art by Frederick Law Olmsted and Calvert Vaux, the park consists of 843 acres of entirely manmade topography and landscape.

The renovation of the Wollman Memorial Rink is an architectural intervention that has helped enormously to turn around public opinion of the park, bringing an influx of new users into what was perceived as a dangerous, crime-ridden place. A project begun decades ago, the site was abandoned due to lack of funds until Donald Trump intervened to save the day. Not exquisitely designed (the rink has been likened to a construction site), it is nonetheless a lovely, romantic spot.

ADDRESS West 59th Street at Sixth Avenue
SUBWAY B, Q to 57th Street N, R to 5th Avenue
BUS M1, M2, M3, M4, M5, M6, M7
ACCESS public

**1986**

Central Park

1986

**Central Park Zoo**

A series of traditional limestone, slate and granite gateways, colonnaded trellises and brick buildings, this zoo is officially titled the 'Central Park Wildlife Conservation Center'. The project replaces the original 1960s zoo, which was both inadequate and inappropriate. Although the replacement seems ecological and humane, and the tiny 5.5-acre site successfully houses a series of satisfying, uncramped displays, it is excruciatingly conservative. An unusual commission for corporate architect Kevin Roche, there was clearly close collaboration with zoo experts.

Reworking the U-shaped plan of the original, the zoo is organised around three zones: tropical, temperate and arctic. Circulation is delightful: the visitors' path leads directly to the exhibits, which house more than 450 animals. The sea lion pool, snow monkey island, red panda forest and multi-level polar bear habitat all provide easy viewing.

And yet this is another example of how frustrating Manhattan architecture has become. This was an opportunity for a new typology, a new form, the use of new materials. None of these was attempted. Nothing about this project dares to be anything but recognisable and familiar. Where is the equivalent of Lubetkin's revolutionary penguin pool at London's Regent's Park zoo?

ADDRESS Fifth Avenue and 64th Street, Central Park
STRUCTURAL ENGINEER Weiskopf & Pickworth
COST $30 million
SIZE 50,000 square feet (4600 square metres)
SUBWAY 6 to 68th Street; B, Q to Lexington Avenue; N, R to 5th Avenue
BUS M1, M2, M3, M4, M66, M72
ACCESS open

**Kevin Roche John Dinkeloo and Associates 1988**

**Kevin Roche John Dinkeloo and Associates 1988**

**Charles A Dana Discovery Center**

The northernmost part of Central Park, situated adjacent to Spanish Harlem, was neglected and underused until recently. During the 1980s the Charles A Dana Foundation (a New York-based philanthropic body) and the Central Park Women's Committee raised much of the funds necessary to erect the Discovery Center, the first phase of a $16-million plan to rehabilitate the 11-acre lake of Harlem Meer. With its water and craggy landscape, this part of the park is now popular with birdwatchers. As part of the project, the North Woods, 200 acres of trees above 96th Street, was cleaned up and reforested and security improvements instituted.

The building is an environmental study centre for schoolchildren. Organised around a cruciform plan, it accommodates a discovery room with interactive exhibits, a wet room allowing access to boats, a classroom, offices and public toilets. A boathouse, sitting half on land and half perched over the Meer, it consists of two pitched-roof rectangles with an adorable cupola in the centre. Composed of brick, granite and bluestone trim, with verge-boards, arches, pendants and brackets mingled with arts-and-crafts gingerbread ornamentation, this pageant of Victoriana was inspired by the work of Frederick Law Olmsted, one of the park's original designers. Not easily recognisable as new (except for its immaculate cleanness), the centre is unobtrusive and unintimidating.

ADDRESS 110th Street near Fifth Avenue, Central Park
STRUCTURAL ENGINEER Weidlinger Associates
COST $1.8 million
SIZE 5200 square feet (483 square metres)
SUBWAY 2, 3, 6 to 110th Street
BUS M1, M2, M3, M4, M18
ACCESS open

Central Park

**Buttrick White & Burtis 1993**

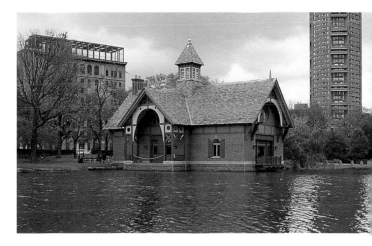

**Central Park**

**Buttrick White & Burtis 1993**

# Upper West Side

**St Thomas Choir School**

This subtle symmetrical street face has been labelled 'contextual'. It is in fact barely noticeable. The wood-framed front entrance and flagpoles have an institutional look, but it is the three-storey framed oriel in the centre of the red-brick façade that starts to hint at the building's contents.

Fifty middle-school choirboys, ages 9 to 14, board, study and rehearse in this vertical campus, America's only church-affiliated choir school. Their 15-storey midtown skyscraper is divided into three sections: the school on the lower six floors; faculty apartments in the middle; and at the 12th floor two towers and a gabled chapel begin. Each part is organised around a series of multi-level double- or triple-height meeting spaces. The division is also visible on the borderline po-mo exterior, where grey decorative banding and quoins demarcate the top of each section.

The small lot, 75 feet by 100 feet, was acquired by St Thomas' in a swap with a local developer. In return for the commercially zoned property of the original site, aid was given in underwriting the cost of the new edifice. The compact new site required several spaces to have a double function. The most ingenious is the gym/rehearsal hall. The building's loads are carried over the underground gymnasium by two-storey trusses. A double layer of sheetrock underneath the coffered ceiling helps create a resonance similiar to St Thomas' stone vaulting. Built-in choir benches on the stage juxtapose amusingly with the basketball court the stage overlooks. Velvet curtains can be lowered to soak up game-time noise.

ADDRESS 202 West 58th Street
STRUCTURAL ENGINEER Weidlinger Associates
SUBWAY 1/9, A, B, C, D to 59th Street/Columbus Circle
BUS M5, M7, M10, M31, M57, M104
ACCESS none

**Upper West Side**

**Buttrick White & Burtis 1987**

**Buttrick White & Burtis 1987**

**Samuel B and David Rose Building, Lincoln Center North**

Lincoln Center for the Performing Arts has often been stamped with perjorative stylistic labels: brutalist, new formalist, fascist. Constructed during the 1960s, its masterplan was created by Wallace K Harrison and the architects involved include Pietro Belluschi, Eero Saarinen, Philip Johnson and SOM. A dated rendition of an Italian piazza, it occupies 14 acres and boasts an unsurpassed profusion of travertine cladding.

Lincoln Center North, the first addition since 1969, provided the opportunity to correct some of the urban-design mistakes of the original. Two new buildings and a reworking of the Juilliard School and Kaskel Plaza have resulted in a more cohesive and urban-friendly place: for instance, the relocation of the Juilliard School's entrance utilises the once-barren promenade one floor above street level.

3 Lincoln Center, a new privately financed 60-storey high-end residential skyscraper designed by Harman Jablin Architects, exploits air rights (purchased for $50 million) over a section of Lincoln Center. The package also required the developers (Stillman Group) to finance the basic structure of the adjacent 28-storey Rose Building, which houses the Walter Reade Film Theater, an experimental theatre, dance studios and dormitory rooms. The relationship between the two towers has been handled with panache: the Rose is clad in cream-coloured Minnesota stone and the apartments are sheathed in black glass.

ADDRESS Amsterdam Avenue and West 65th Street
COST $150 million SIZE 350,000 square feet (32,500 square metres)
SUBWAY 1 to 66th Street
BUS M5, M7, M11, M66, M72, M104
ACCESS concourse and lobby open

Upper West Side

**Davis, Brody & Associates 1990**

**Iridium**

One of J W von Goethe's most famous observations is that architecture is frozen music. Designer Jordan Mozer has attempted to realise this notion by creating an architecture that is music frozen at the point at which it is beginning to solidify. Iridium, an explosively vibrant restaurant, is according to Mozer, 'what music would look like if you could see it'. One is not sure that this is quite what Goethe had in mind: it seems that there are many different melodies and rhythms playing simultaneously in this complex eatery.

Lincoln Center (see page 230), located directly across the street, was the point of inspiration for this cacophonous space. Mozer imagined the essence of the performing arts floating out of the Lincoln Center complex and crystallising into the form of Iridium. There are literal references to well-known stars: the Placido Domingo column sports a tuxedo and tails and expands visually as though it might be about to burst into song; the extraordinary façade is framed in stainless steel and topped by five curlicued copper roofs, three of which are titled 'Baryshnikov roofs' as they are meant to be leaping over one another. General metaphors abound too: settees perform a *pas de deux* while a cabinet is standing in ballet's third position.

The hilarious furniture is the most successful element of this design. An orange BellBottom chair shod in platform shoes sits near a moulded-aluminium Ballerina chair complete with legwarmers. Bronze and blown-glass table lamps pirouette in tutus. Metal handrails are formed from intertwined notes fashioned after clarinet hardware. This is an animated dreamland, occasionally becoming so overrun with fanciful notions that it turns into hysteria, a nightmare.

Mozer approaches his work as pure, seamless fantasy. The lack of a hierarchy of ideas adds to the surreal aspect. Undulating walls, an

**Jordan Mozer & Associates 1994**

**Upper West Side**

Jordan Mozer & Associates 1994

emphasis on narrative, decorative details (such as doors wearing copper Band-Aids where they get might scuffed) create a cartoonish atmosphere. Ridiculous scale, juxtapositions, psychedelic colours and beautifully crafted finishes make one feel as though one is mired in an episode of *The Jetsons* on Ecstasy.

ADDRESS 44 West 63rd Street
COST $1.8 million
SIZE 8700 square feet (810 square metres)
SUBWAY 1/9 to 66th Street; A, B, C, D to 59th Street/Columbus Circle
BUS M5, M7, M10
ACCESS open

**Jordan Mozer & Associates 1994**

**Jordan Mozer & Associates 1994**

# ABC Studios

The design evolution of Kohn Pedersen Fox can be witnessed in this tiny pocket of Manhattan. ABC was the practice's first client in 1976 and the two companies have continued a fruitful relationship. Five major projects designed by KPF for ABC sit within a two-block radius.

The first, completed in 1978, is the restoration and conversion into television studios of the grand Battery Armory (dating from 1905) on 66th Street. The first new building is an unremarkable limestone, brick and glass tower at 30 West 67th Street, designed in 1979. WABC Studios, also completed in 1979, is more noteworthy. The windowless brick and terracotta box has a glass lobby wrapping around the corner and a three-storey glazed atrium at the top.

47 West 66th Street, completed in 1986, is a study model of contextual post-modernism. A six-storey base maintains the street wall; the heavy square tower above is alleviated by large semicircular bays. Capital Cities at 77 West 66th Street – a 22-storey office tower angling to appear residential – is unobtrusive yet irritating. The most recent addition, at 147 Columbus Avenue, is perhaps the least attractive of all. Heavy brick massing and a top layer of six storeys of black glass seem oppressive. Essentially two rectangular volumes that intersect with a faceted curtain wall, the proportions seem out of whack. A gestural mast signalling ABC's presence only adds further confusion to the façade.

ADDRESS 47 West 66th Street; 77 West 66th Street; 147 Columbus Avenue
STRUCTURAL ENGINEER Weiskopf & Pickworth; Severud-Szegezdy; Severud Associates
SUBWAY 1/9 to 66th Street; B, C to 72nd Street
BUS M7, M10, M11, M66, M72
ACCESS none

**Kohn Pedersen Fox Associates 1986, 1988, 1992**

**Kohn Pedersen Fox Associates 1986, 1988, 1992**

**Lincoln Square Sony Theater**

The context of post-urban Manhattan as the site for this suburban freak is inexplicable. The kitsch, overscaled architecture and tacky theme-park interior of this vulgar vertical film mall is disturbing.

The only saving grace is the glittery multiplex's unabashed relationship with Broadway. A section of the heavy exterior is a glass curtain wall that becomes part of the street at night. From the outside, one can glimpse the complex's art-deco carpet, neo-classical festoons and a 75-foot-high mural honouring the immortals of Hollywood's golden age. Once inside, after negotiating a poorly planned lobby and riding the narrow escalators, the concession area is reached through a facsimile of a Sony studio gate in Culver City. One is immediately struck by the disconcerting image of unimaginably crass giant golden palm trees. The entryways to all 12 cinemas are Disney versions of famous movie-palace façades, complete with titles: Avalon, Valencia, Capitol, Majestic. Moroccan themes, Egyptian sphinxes, Mayan-temple archways and plaster pagodas are gaudily arrayed on these entrances. I fail to see any successful translation of 1920s and 1930s white-tie glamour.

Despite the embarrassingly gauche architecture, New Yorkers seem to love the space for its comfort – at weekends one must book tickets well in advance.

ADDRESS 1998 Broadway
CLIENT Sony Theatres
STRUCTURAL ENGINEER Entertainment Engineering
SUBWAY 1/9 to 66th Street; B, C to 72nd Street
BUS M5, M7, M11, M66, M72, M104
ACCESS open

**Upper West Side**

**Gensler and Associates (in LA) 1995**

**Gensler and Associates (in LA) 1995**

# 353 Central Park West

Replacing three vacant late-19th-century rowhouses, this new 19-storey corner apartment building lies at the heart of the Upper West Side/Central Park West Historic District. The design team therefore had to please many influential camps: the Landmarks Preservation Commission, West Side community groups, the Municipal Art Society, and the Historic Buildings Committee of the NYC AIA. A pre-design report had to be prepared analysing elements intrinsic to the celebrated luxury residences along Central Park West: materials, colours, massing, entrances, fenestration, and decorative embellishments down to plant tubs.

A major topic of discussion was the setbacks occurring on buildings along the street. To create this popular cascading effect, 353 meets the street wall at ground plane, rising to a 150-foot cornice level. A series of stepped-back terraces then recedes from both the avenue and street elevations, resulting in a turret-topped penthouse and watertower.

The condominium floorplans are as conservative as the building exterior. One apartment per floor (there are only 16 in total) allows reiterative elements to be expressed on the façades. Inside, marble entryways, maids' quarters, rosewood floors and woodburning fireplaces set the tone. The views over Central Park are stunning.

ADDRESS 353 Central Park West
CLIENT KISKA Developers
ARCHITECT OF RECORD The Vilkas Group
STRUCTURAL ENGINEER The Office of Irwin G Cantor
SUBWAY B, C to 66th Street
BUS M10, M96
ACCESS none

**Upper West Side**

**Yorgancioglu Architects 1992**

**Yorgancioglu Architects 1992**

# Morningside Heights
# and Harlem

# Columbia University Computer Science Building

Chartered in 1754, Columbia – one of eight topnotch Ivy League universities – is one of America's oldest educational institutions. Fitting snugly into Manhattan's urban grid, its campus stretches from West 114th Street to West 120th Street and from Broadway to Amsterdam Avenue. A McKim, Mead & White masterplan drawn up in 1893 resulted in the magnificent Low Library, a few courtyards and the odd Beaux-Arts classroom. The rest of the largely Italian Renaissance campus (red brick and limestone with copper roofs) developed piecemeal, made up of individual buildings of varying degrees of architectural merit. It is a treat to wander through this dense, higgledy-piggledy metropolitan tableau.

The Computer Science Building is in the north-east corner of the campus. The rooftop site, which once accommodated the Bloomingdale Asylum for the Insane, is surrounded by buildings ranging in date from 1897 to 1958. Functioning as a connector between three separate structures, a public courtyard and the street, the new addition succeeds beautifully in its clever manipulation of very different interlocking spaces. According to the husband-and-wife architectural team (both Columbia alumni and currently professors at the School of Architecture), 'The building organizes the disparate elements of the context into a coherent whole and the building is in turn completed by them.' Their hybrid of new construction and reconstruction plays with notions of negative and positive. The courtyard organises the entire project, both ceremonially and functionally. The aesthetic – 'a balance, appropriate to circumstances, of elements of classical, vernacular, and modernist origins' – is modest, graceful and subdued.

The building's detailing is beautiful, articulations are clean and the overall form is quietly elegant. The limestone street façade has classical

**R M Kliment & Frances Halsband Architects 1983**

**R M Kliment & Frances Halsband Architects 1983**

proportions achieved with rythmically placed polished-granite pilasters, recessed windows and spandrels. These windows are in fact fakes: blue-stone panels masquerading as fenestration provide yet another play on negative and positive, solid and void, reality and illusion.

A delightful subversive quality pervades this rigorous intellectual architecture.

ADDRESS Amsterdam Avenue
STRUCTURAL ENGINEER Robert Silman Associates
COST $3.9 million
SIZE 38,000 square feet (3500 square metres)
SUBWAY 1/9 to 116th Street
BUS M4, M5, M11, M60, M104
ACCESS none

**R M Kliment & Frances Halsband Architects 1983**

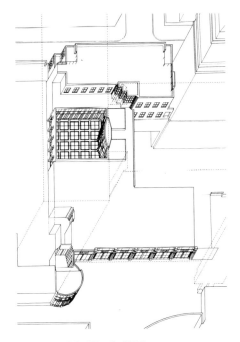

**R M Kliment & Frances Halsband Architects 1983**

# Columbia University Uris Hall Addition

The original Uris Hall, housing Columbia's Business School, was built in 1964. An eight-storey glass and metal building, its brutalist aesthetic was never popular on campus. The new addition, though well received by critics, is also something of a misfit. Brutally po-mo, pompous and oppressive, it envelops the front of the original edifice by fitting between the existing three-storey wings and granite stairs. Although it doesn't hide the old structure completely, it is so overpowering one forgets what is behind it. The limestone-clad façade is punctuated by recessed fenestration set in a double pattern of large 9-by-9 squares.

The interior is equally irritating. Self-important twin bluestone staircases with big concrete balls at either end rise from a lobby with a marble-studded terrazzo floor. Hermes, the Greek god of commerce, is engraved at the end of the vestibule. The imposing effect was perhaps intentional since Columbia's students conduct job interviews here with visiting potential employers. But I question the need for such a brazenly corporate building on this leafy collegiate campus.

The addition is cleverly engineered, though. Sitting on top of an old gymnasium and boiler room, a two-storey truss resting on four 60-foot columns supports the entire structure.

ADDRESS North campus, north of Low Library
STRUCTURAL ENGINEER DeSimone, Chaplin & Associates
SIZE 30,000 square feet (2800 square metres)
SUBWAY 1/9 to 116th Street
BUS M4, M5, M11, M60, M104
ACCESS lobby open

**Peter L Gluck & Partners 1986**

**Peter L Gluck & Partners 1986**

# Barnard College Sulzberger Hall

The elegant contemporary contextualism of this building makes it instantly recognisable as a Polshek project. The flag, clock and belltower of the roofscape are familiar themes in his work. Nautical pastiche is clearly a favourite inspiration. Surprisingly, it actually works well on Manhattan's Upper West Side.

The edifice is divided into two parts: a 20-storey tower and an L-shaped 'midrise' that is the same height as the existing dorms. The material of the tower – Flemish-bond brickwork – relates to the existing buildings and the project's eight-storey wings harmonise with their surroundings through their massing.

This subtle skyscraper tells a different story from different vantage points. From afar the tower functions as a campanile, yet on the street the fenestration and materials give clues to the programme. Metal and glass demarcate the public areas while the residential suites are clad in brick and stone. The brickwork also links the new building to the affiliated Columbia University across the street.

The dorm tower encloses a residential courtyard on Lehman Lawn, replacing what was an unformed open space with a secure and private quad. The view of the building from the lawn is truly architectonic: vertical sections of masonry sandwich a metal and glass sliver. The strictly geometric fenestration creates a soothing pattern, making this an eminently readable building.

ADDRESS 3009 Broadway
STRUCTURAL ENGINEER The Office of Irwin G Cantor
SUBWAY 1/9 to 116th Street
BUS M4, M5, M11, M60, M104
ACCESS none

**James Stewart Polshek and Partners Architects 1988**

**James Stewart Polshek and Partners Architects 1988**

**Dance Theater of Harlem**

The Dance Theater of Harlem was founded almost 30 years ago in the basement of a local church. The former parking-garage site on which it now stands was first converted by Hardy Holzman Pfeiffer in 1971. Expanded and transformed in 1994, the building now serves as the headquarters for an internationally acclaimed professional company of 50 dancers and a school attended by 1300 students. Located on a street composed primarily of tenements and municipal buildings, this unabashedly proud edifice has brought an influx of upbeat interest to the area. Its close proximity to a local playground gives the building corner exposure, allowing visibility from a number of vantage points.

In a homage to founder Arthur Mitchell, a weathervane in his image leaps joyously in the wind atop the building. This spirit of exuberance is reflected throughout the design. The architects were inspired by the building's function to treat the structure as a choreographed event. Colour on both exterior and interior adds vibrancy: the dynamic exterior juxtaposes red brick, black and white horizontally striped ceramic masonry and synthetic shingles. A curved roof crowns the main volume, adding to the syncopated quality of the project.

Inside, the expansion required the cutting of passageways through loadbearing brick walls and the addition of steel columns for support.

ADDRESS 466 West 152nd Street
STRUCTURAL ENGINEER Peter Galdi
COST $4.5 million
SIZE 28,000 square feet (2600 square metres)
SUBWAY 1/9 to 137th Street/City College; B, C to 135th Street
BUS M3, M11, M18
ACCESS open

**Morningside Heights and Harlem**

**Hardy Holzman Pfeiffer Associates 1994**

**Hardy Holzman Pfeiffer Associates 1994**

# Riverbank State Park

Richard Dattner describes the delicate process of negotiation and decision-making that led to the creation of Riverbank State Park as 'architectural triage': a question of working with 'choices, priorities and the determination of what will yield the greatest good for the greatest number'.

In 1965 a federal court order was issued requiring New York City to process all raw sewage before unloading it into the Hudson River. The site chosen for the processing plant for all sewage from the West Side was in Harlem. This caused much upset among the local community, who feared unpleasant/unhealthy odours. As a consolation, Nelson Rockefeller, the then governor, offered a green recreational park on top of the plant. Richard Dattner was selected as designer of the park in 1979 by a committee made up of state officials and community representatives. A nine-year process of community board meetings, document preparation and several cycles of design and redesign finally resulted in the park as it appears today.

Situated on top of the 28-acre North River Pollution Treatment Plant, the park is linked to the neighbourhood by vehicular/pedestrian bridges at West 138th and West 145th Streets. Dattner describes the park as being 'on a strict diet because of the limited loadbearing capacity of the plant's caissons, columns and roof spans'.

All building loads had to be transferred to columns resting directly on the columns that support the plant. Therefore the overall plan of the park was dictated by the plant's existing structural system. The North River Pollution Treatment Plant is constructed of 14 separate sections which move independently as the 6-foot-deep precast-concrete roof expands and contracts due to temperature fluctuations. To further complicate matters, each section has a different load capacity. Landscaping and

**Richard Dattner Architect 1991**

**Richard Dattner Architect 1991**

paving, both uniformly supported loads, rest level on the roof. All the park structures are fabricated from lightweight steel with metal or tile-faced panels as the primary wall systems.

The buildings (which include a cultural centre, a skating rink, a restaurant and a gymnasium) are organised around a central courtyard with a continuous waterside promenade ringing the perimeter.

ADDRESS West 137th Street to West 145th Street west of the Henry Hudson Parkway to the Hudson River
CLIENT State of New York
LANDSCAPE ARCHITECT Abel, Bainnson, Butz
STRUCTURAL ENGINEER Ewell W Finley
COST $130 million
SUBWAY 1/9 to 137 Street or 145 Street
BUS M11, BX19
ACCESS open

**Richard Dattner Architect 1991**

**Richard Dattner Architect 1991**

# Bronx

# Hostos Community College, East Academic Complex

Hostos Community College is located on the once elegant main boulevard of the Bronx. Today, only a school and a WPA-era post office serve as reminders of the district's golden age. Hostos serves a mostly low-income, Hispanic population. The majority of students are women, of whom 60 per cent are single heads of households; many arrive as recipients of welfare but after two years of study have the skills necessary to earn middle-class salaries. Founded 25 years ago and named after the Puerto Rican educator Eugenio Maria de Hostos, the campus is on the site of a former tyre factory. The new building houses a student lounge, cafeteria, gymnasium and auditorium, and a prominent art gallery.

The complex is organised around a skylit pedestrian bridge which functions as an informal meeting point. The exterior is not remarkable: its contextual massing, materials and colour make it disappear into its urban setting. The internal central spine and central circulation space is a five-storey skylit atrium, articulated vertically by cantilevered stairs and defined horizontally by balconies. Functional, durable materials are alleviated by po-mo geometries: squares are repeated as interior fenestration and a green grid pattern appears on the floor. The furniture is playful, slightly out of character with the practical ambience. Giant elliptical marble benches set on wheels are strategically placed throughout.

ADDRESS 500 Grand Concourse, Bronx
STRUCTURAL ENGINEER The Cantor Seinuk Group
SIZE 240,000 square feet (22,300 square metres)
SUBWAY 2, 4, 5 to 149th Street/Grand Concourse
BUS BX1, BX19
ACCESS open

**Bronx**

**Gwathmey Siegel & Associates Architects 1993**

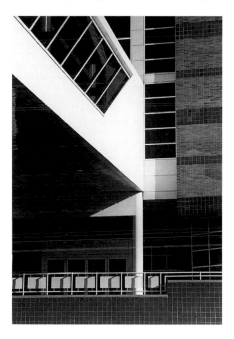

Bronx

**Gwathmey Siegel & Associates Architects 1993**

# Sedgwick Branch Library

Exterior form expresses internal function in this small public library. Two clear geometries, articulated using dissimilar materials, were chosen to differentiate the two programmatic requirements.

An L-shaped plan with a half in-half out cone sits on an awkward triangular lot. The main reading spaces are accommodated in a narrow rectilinear concrete volume that fronts the main boulevard. A long skylit gallery opens on to an external plaza to the north which in turn leads to the main circulation system of the building.

Meeting this rectilinear mass outdoors is a 15-foot stainless-steel cone which houses public functions and community activities. A steel stud structure, the cone was clad first with timber and then cloaked with wedge-shaped panels of mill-finished stainless steel. David Prendergast has called this element 'a giant teepee' and claims that the circular form was an attempt to spotlight community togetherness. Certainly the very visible cone gives the library a clear identity in the neighbourhood.

The residual lot has been meticulously landscaped by artist Sandy Geller. Contoured concrete steps are punctuated by brass etched bollards which glow in the dark in a formation based on the Sigma Galaxy. Mica rocks have been lodged in the waving pavement. A bit stark, the entire project has a moonscape feel.

The Sedgwick neighbourhood is undergoing renewal and the new library is seen as a significant step in the community's revitalisation.

ADDRESS 1701 University Avenue, Bronx
STRUCTURAL ENGINEER Stanley H Goldstein
COST $1.2 million SIZE 4000 square feet (370 square metres)
SUBWAY 4 to 176 Street BUS BX3, BX18, BX36
ACCESS open

Bronx

**David W Prendergast Architects 1993**

Bronx

**David W Prendergast Architects 1993**

# Lehman College Physical Education Facility

This project is about roof. Not merely its own roof, but an exploration of the many roles a structure that forms the top of a building may play. Roof as topography and typology: landscape, shelter, wall and gateway. Mill-finished stainless-steel planes curve fluidly over exposed trusses to form this extraordinary covering; the aerodynamic materials and sloping form exude a gentle power. In a clever balancing act, the internally exposed structure exaggerates the notion of the building as athlete, while simultaneously the hill-like exterior reinforces the notion of the building as geography.

Steel-reinforced concrete foundations support a superstructure of steel box trusses spanning 101 feet. The roof cantilevers 10 feet over the exposed structure, shading the indoor swimming pool and two gymnasiums sited one floor below grade. The building runs the entire length of the campus' longitudinal axis. The steel is interrupted periodically by longitudinal windows and a break occurs where an aluminium and glass skylight covers the central public corridor.

The facility was designed as a gateway between the community and the college campus. Defining the campus' north edge, the street front is precast concrete with a well-monitored courtyard entrance. This is at the level of the spectator seating adjacent to locker facilities that link the building's components.

ADDRESS Bedford Park Boulevard West, Bronx
STRUCTURAL ENGINEER Severud & Associates
COST $40 million SIZE 165,000 square feet (15,300 square metres)
SUBWAY 4 to Bedford Park Blvd BUS BX26, BX28
ACCESS none

**Rafael Viñoly Architects 1994**

Bronx

**Bronx**

**Rafael Viñoly Architects 1994**

# Queens

# Isamu Noguchi Garden Museum

The Japanese-American sculptor and designer Isamu Noguchi believed that 'the senses are tactile, not informational or verbal'. In this museum devoted to his work it is impossible to quash the desire to touch: the exquisite sculptures, the textured watermarks on the floor, the apple trees, and the remarkably still water flowing from a fountain. Much of Noguchi's work is about opposites – smooth/rough, solid/hollow, natural/manmade – and here new additions are juxtaposed with the existing fabric, indoor with outdoor and art with its environment.

Located in an industrial neighbourhood, the fortress-like exterior reveals next to nothing about its contents. Noguchi rehabilitated this two-storey brick photographic-chemicals warehouse, added a cement-block structure and filled the site's triangular form with a rock garden. In a wilful hybrid of exterior and interior, brick walls do not terminate but extend into the garden, the first gallery space is roofless, and so on. Open windows have been strategically cut through thick walls to allow views of Manhattan to mingle with the rain and the indoor birch trees. Through elegant spatial manipulation, the visitor is led around 14 separate gallery areas. The route is cyclical and one may circulate again and again. The museum's atmosphere is cool and contemplative, movingly tranquil.

Among Noguchi's public works are the sculpture courtyard at 1 Chase Manhattan Plaza, the arcaded water wall at 666 Fifth Avenue, the façade of the Associated Press Building (Rockefeller Plaza between 50th and 51st in Rockefeller Center) and the vermilion *Cube* at 140 Broadway.

ADDRESS 32–7 Vernon Blvd, Long Island City, Queens
SUBWAY B, Q to 21st Street; N to 36th Street
BUS Q103, Q104
ACCESS open to the public April through November; call before

**Isamu Noguchi and Shoji Sadao 1985**

**Isamu Noguchi and Shoji Sadao 1985**

**American Museum of the Moving Image**

Liberal expanses of barium yellow and vermilion red energise this grey neighbourhood. A blocky, volumetric façade with intersecting angles and curves contrasts greatly with the surrounding warehouse sheds. Visible from the expressway, the bright exterior is enticing, drawing the potential visitor closer. All this jazzy sunshine occurs at the rear of the building.

The original building is part of the legendary Paramount Studios. Silent-era greats Rudolph Valentino, Gloria Swanson, W C Fields and the Marx Brothers all made films here. The three-storey loft housing the museum is listed on the National Register of Historic Places, inhibiting any changes to the front façade. Gwathmey Siegel placed a new stair and elevator tower on axis with the main entrance, creating a graceful and transparent counterpoint to the symmetrical gridded masonry street façade and gaining greater floor capacity inside.

According to the architects, the stairs are 'the iconic object … orienting the entire complex'. Cantilevered from the elevator core, the concrete stairway is enclosed in tinted laminated-glass panels framed by white steel joists. The articulation of the junctions between old and new is deliberately exaggerated.

ADDRESS 35th Avenue and 36th Street, Astoria, Queens
STRUCTURAL ENGINEER Severud Szegezdy
SIZE 35,000 square feet (3250 square metres)
SUBWAY G to Steinway Street; N to 39th Street/Beebe Avenue
BUS Q66, Q101, Q102
ACCESS open

**Gwathmey Siegel & Associates Architects 1988**

Queens

Queens

**Gwathmey Siegel & Associates Architects 1988**

**Citicorp at Court Square**

The tallest building outside Manhattan, this lofty silver tower is visible from far and wide. The only skyscraper in Queens, it is planned on a direct axis with the midtown Manhattan Citicorp building. Sitting on a 2-acre residential site surrounded by landmarked avenues and a small park, this 50-storey edifice is an odd insertion into a historic neighbourhood. Blocky and chunky, it has a serene quality as it stands alone on a quiet village street.

Constructed of a glass-spandrel curtain wall enveloping pale-green metal panels, the tower has dramatic graduated corner setbacks at the highest floors. The entrance plaza – a seven-storey glass rotunda enclosing a pedestrian concourse – is accessible from two subway stations. This undeground skylit atrium is decorated with the expected plethora of indoor plants and a noisy waterfall. That a 663-foot tower was planned with a below-ground entrance was clearly an architectural gesture to emphasise the building's connection with its Manhattan sibling. A subway line runs directly from the original Citicorp at Lexington Avenue and East 53rd Street to this Queens site.

ADDRESS 44th Drive and 45th Avenue, Queens
SIZE 1.4 million square feet (130,000 square metres)
ACCESS atrium and lobby open

**Skidmore, Owings & Merrill 1989**

Queens

**Skidmore, Owings & Merrill 1989**

# Queens County Criminal Court

Three additions have been made to an existing courthouse as part of a phased plan. The ultimate goal is to consolidate the Queens County Criminal Justice facilities into one complex. The new additions – a new entrance, a public plaza and an east wing – accommodate ten new courts, centralised clerks' offices, police secure lock-up and space for the probation department. Security considerations were paramount, so the site was organised around secure courtyards which contain gated, landscaped parking for judges and allow views for adjoining offices. The desire to reflect the green, suburban nature of Queens was important.

As described by the architects, this project entailed 'taking a bland and offputting building and making it better'. The 1950s structure lacked a civic presence. The new, sombre but smart edifice is a decidedly decent building – contemporary and tasteful – with a surprisingly friendly character. The additions envelop the old building, successfully integrating old and new so that it is almost impossible to tell where the two meet.

The site is visible directly off Queens Blvd and Van Wyck Expressway, creating the need for an automobile-scale presence: a contemporary suburban design consideration met by a large green glass curved element.

A kinetic structure by Japanese sculptor Susumu Shingu stands outside the lobby. The cyclical movements of this large, circular stainless-steel work are intended as a metaphor for individuality within the restrictions of a system of law, either nature's or society's.

ADDRESS 125–01 Queens Boulevard
SUBWAY F to Van Wyck
BUS Q60
ACCESS lobby open; public access to courtrooms

**Queens**

**Ehrenkrantz & Eckstut Architects**

**Ehrenkrantz & Eckstut Architects**

# Queens Museum Reconstruction

New York City Parks Commissioner from 1934 to 1960, Robert Moses was responsible for the construction of 14 freeways, over 400 miles of parkway, seven major bridges, tens of thousands of public housing units, 658 playgrounds, the UN headquarters, Lincoln Center, the New York Coliseum, Shea Stadium, Co-op City and Jones Beach. A visionary mega-lomaniac, Moses is today attributed with positive creations as well as a great many urban mistakes.

'Robert Moses was, for almost half a century, the single most powerful man of our time in New York, the shaper not only of the city's politics but of its physical structure,' states Robert Caro in his biography of Moses, *The Power Broker*. 'He personally conceived and completed public works costing $27 billion dollars – the greatest builder America (and probably the world) has ever known.'

Appointed as president of the 1964/65 World's Fair Corporation, Moses commissioned an enormous three-dimensional scale model of the 320 square miles of New York City's five boroughs. An eight-minute tracked-car ride, advertised as 'the helicopter trip', took visitors around the perimeter of the metropolis. Covering 9335 square feet, the model is at a scale of 1 inch to 100 feet and authentically duplicates topography as well as architecture.

Intended for use as an urban-planning tool after the fair, it never lived up to expectations. The property of the Triborough Bridge & Tunnel Authority, it recently underwent two years of renovation by its original manufacturer, Lester Associates. Eight hundred thousand miniature buildings were increased with 95,000 additions.

A must-see for anyone with an interest in cities, the model is superb. A rising glass-bottomed ramp leads one around it, providing the complete range of vantage points. Changing from artificial sunlight to nightscape,

**Rafael Viñoly Architects 1994**

**Rafael Viñoly Architects 1994**

the entire model glows in the dark. A moving aeroplane lands once a minute at the diminutive La Guardia airport. Giving a glorious bird's-eye view, the model imparts a sense of the scope, scale and density of the Big Apple.

The exhibition space for the model was redesigned by Rafael Viñoly Architects as part of the complete reconstruction of the Queens Museum, built originally for the 1939 World's Fair. The programme required the reintegration of the museum and the park, achieved by extending the east façade of the existing edifice and creating a new formal entry facing the park. This entry incorporates a 17-foot-diameter aluminium revolving door and skylight placed on a symmetrical axis with the Unisphere – a 380-ton stainless-steel spherical sculpture of the earth and its orbiting satellites. Standing 12 storeys high on a 70-ton, 20-foot-high steel base, the Unisphere is a Queens mascot.

The north façade of the museum was redesigned to accommodate a secondary entrance for staff and reclad in precast-concrete panels to match the existing limestone. An 18-foot cantilevered glass and steel canopy covers this entry.

The museum interior, now a flowing, engaging series of spaces, was designed to be 'flexible, functionally clear and aesthetically neutral', according to the architects.

ADDRESS Flushing Meadow, Corona Park
CLIENT New York City Department of General Services
SUBWAY 7 to Willets Point
BUS Q23, Q58, Q88
ACCESS open

**Queens**

**Rafael Viñoly Architects 1994**

**Rafael Viñoly Architects 1994**

# Brooklyn

**Rotunda Gallery**

Named after its original site, the rotunda of Brooklyn's Borough Hall, the non-profit-making Rotunda Gallery is now located on the street level of an office building in Brooklyn Heights. The design is playfully aware of the relationship between the observer and the observed. The definition and position of gallery components aims to encourage engagement through overlap: the stair/viewing balcony, the moving door/wall.

An extraordinary flexibility has been achieved. The main organisational element is a two-storey pivoting partition wall that swivels along a steel arc embedded in the concrete floor. When the wall is open, the entry platform allows a full view of the gallery. When partially open, the wall becomes a door and blocks access, altering the surrounding spaces.

An exhibition bridge leads to the office mezzanine. The concrete stairs leading to this bridge have a dual-purpose maple strip inserted into one step, enabling the attachment of displays and demarcating 65 inches above the floor, the optimal mounting line for art. The translucent plexiglass railing contrasts beautifully with the raw concrete steps. The materials throughout – concrete, light maple plywood, steel, lexan, cast aluminium – add to the streamlined, clean atmosphere. The uplighting has been designed to create the illusion of a forced perspective, making the space appear larger than it is. There is a light, floating quality to this lovely space, a serenity that lends itself well to the display of art.

ADDRESS 33 Clinton Street, Brooklyn Heights
SIZE 1600 square feet (150 square metres)
SUBWAY 2, 3, 4, 5 to Borough Hall; A, C, F to Jay Street/Borough Hall; M, N, R to Court Street
BUS B25, B26, B38, B41, B51, B52
ACCESS open

Brooklyn

**Smith-Miller + Hawkinson Architects 1993**

**Brooklyn**

**Smith-Miller + Hawkinson Architects 1993**

**Brooklyn Law School**

This 11-storey tower of precast concrete and limestone is in fact an addition to an existing 1968 building. The first nine floors, containing student and faculty facilities, are attached to the original building; the two top, unconnected floors are a formal dining space and a library.

This is a faintly post-modern, stalwartly contextual building that sits on a superb site. Downtown Brooklyn is a conglomeration of grand historic structures, mostly in Greek revival style. Once America's third-largest city, Brooklyn did not get swallowed up by Manhattan until the two were amalgamated in 1898.

Robert Stern: 'This solution was about fitting into the context, which I saw as defined by the various kinds of classical architecture around it.' A fairly bland edifice, the law school blends so well into its surroundings it is almost at risk of disappearing.

ADDRESS 250 Joralemon Street, Brooklyn Heights
ASSOCIATE ARCHITECTS Wank Adams Slavin Associates
COST $25 million
SIZE 90,000 square feet (8400 square metres)
SUBWAY 2, 3, 4, 5 to Borough Hall; A, C, F to Jay Street/Borough Hall; M, N, R to Court Street
BUS B25, B26, B37, B38, B45, B51, B52, B65, B75
ACCESS none

**Robert A M Stern 1994**

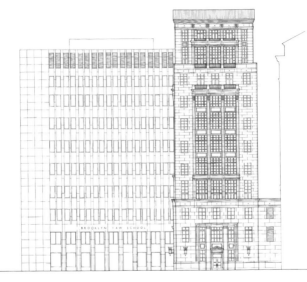

**Robert A M Stern 1994**

# The BAM Majestic Theater

Stepping into this theatre is like entering a bizarrely squeaky-clean ancient ruin. Behind shiny new, dark-green doors is a wonderful combination of old and new, cleaned-up and distressed surfaces. The original theatre, constructed in 1903, seated 1700 and was famous as the audition hall for Gershwin musicals. Abandoned in 1968 as a result of changing demographics, this once grand space slipped into a state of disrepair.

The renovation included a great deal of spatial reconfiguration. The architects turned a formal, turn-of-the-century plan into a more intimate experience. The existing theatre was three tiered, had conventional railings on the boxes, two balconies and a proscenium. Hardy Holzman Pfeiffer raised the stage and orchestra one grade so audience and stage are on the same level. The mezzanine was removed, reducing the seating capacity to 900. The funky new seating – upholstered benches and high stools with backrests – makes a pleasant change from plush velvet chairs.

The lobby space is the original and its decay has been wittily glorified. The richly coloured wall layers, exposed by peeling plaster and scarred by watermarks, have been left intact. Areas of random natural decay have been joined by indiscernible freshly replastered and predistressed areas. Exposed steelwork was fireproofed, painted and left as exposed. The space is rich with a tangible historic layering.

ADDRESS 30 Lafayette Avenue, Fort Greene, Brooklyn
CLIENT The Brooklyn Academy of Music
STRUCTURAL ENGINEER Purdy & Henderson Associates
COST $5 million
SUBWAY 2, 3, 4, 5, D, Q, to Atlantic Avenue; A, C to Lafayette Avenue; B, M, N, R to Pacific; G to Fulton Street BUS B25, B26, B38, B52
ACCESS open

Brooklyn

**Hardy Holzman Pfeiffer Associates 1987**

Brooklyn

**Hardy Holzman Pfeiffer Associates 1987**

# Brooklyn Museum Addition and Masterplan

Planned as a 25-year undertaking, it is hoped this expansion will be completed by the second decade of the 21st century. A surprising team of collaborators was selected through an invitation-only architectural competition held in 1986. James Stewart Polshek and Partners and Arata Isozaki & Associates were chosen from five eminent semi-finalists. The two firms teamed up because the competition required affiliation with a firm licensed in New York State.

Both practices had pertinent yet different areas of expertise. Polshek brought prose to the project and Isozaki poetry. The winning scheme, which proposes an expansion to the south elevation, includes a new sculpture garden, restaurant, terraces and formal stairs linking the museum to the adjacent Prospect Park. A 150-foot-high obelisk destined for the centre of the existing museum was inspired by McKim, Mead & White's original 1893 masterplan, which was never completed. The winning scheme was said to have 'an appropriate scale of monumentality'.

Planned in a total of ten phases, only the first is currently finished. Consisting of a new art-storage facility, a new auditorium and the renovation of the entire West Wing, its showpiece is undoubtedly the auditorium. Located on the third floor of a 1970s extension designed by Prentice & Chan, Olhausen, it was an unfinished exhibition space for years. Now a dignified 460-seat, 10,000-square-foot lecture hall, its most remarkable feature is its extraordinary ceiling.

The undulating surface is both unusual and beautiful. Designed as a series of hyperbolic paraboloids (sine curves moving in two directions), special technology was required to construct it. A grid was superimposed on the ceiling plan and calculations from point to point were documented. This deformed grid was actually used during construction, defined by a

**Arata Isozaki & Assocs/James Stewart Polshek and Partners 1992**

**Arata Isozaki & Assocs/James Stewart Polshek and Partners 1992**

laser beam. Metal-mesh framework was installed first and then the ceiling was finished by master craftsmen using a plaster-on-wire lathe technique. Perforated stainless-steel panels, stainless-steel stairs and 6000 square feet of vertically slip-matched oak panelling, all cut from a single tree, on the rear of the stage and walls blend tightly together. A tantalising taste of what is to come.

ADDRESS 200 Eastern Parkway, Crown Heights
STRUCTURAL ENGINEER Robert Silman Associates
COST $17.5 million
SIZE 52,600 square feet (4900 square metres)
SUBWAY 2, 3 to Eastern Parkway
BUS BX 71
ACCESS open

**Brooklyn**

**Arata Isozaki & Assocs/James Stewart Polshek and Partners 1992**

Brooklyn

**Arata Isozaki & Assocs/James Stewart Polshek and Partners 1992**

# Steinhardt Conservatory

A lovely, tranquil oasis, the conservatory is an enchanting set of buildings, sparkling in sunlight and glowing at night. Sited along the outer perimeter of the Brooklyn Botanic Gardens (masterplanned by Frederick Law Olmsted in 1910), these transparent treasure troves create a buffer between nature and the city, streetscape and landscape.

Treated and titled as a single structure, the conservatory is in fact composed of four individual parts: a linear building adjacent to Washington Avenue with three separate octagonal pavilions set in front. The neo-Victorian tubular-steel and glass greenhouses take some design cues from the nearby Palm House (renamed the Steinhardt Conservatory), designed in 1918 by McKim, Mead & White and virtually reconstructed by Davis, Brody & Associates. Its oval, curvaceous form is offset by the angular, rectilinear configuration of the newer structures.

The three two-level pavilions are linked by an underground circular gallery. Each is crowned by a central cupola. The steel structural framework has been painted a soft green on the exterior and a bold white on the interior. This structural shell holds horizontal glass panels, a contemporary take on the more customary vertical panelling. Outdoor stairways connect with various garden paths. Entering each pavilion from the lower level is quite dramatic, the spectacular plant worlds unfolding as one moves upward. Once inside what are essentially containers, one's focal point appropriately switches to the exhibits.

ADDRESS The Brooklyn Botanic Gardens, 1000 Washington Avenue
STRUCTURAL ENGINEER Goldreich, Page & Thropp
COST $25 million
SUBWAY 2, 3 to Eastern Parkway BUS BX 71
ACCESS open

**Brooklyn**

**Davis, Brody & Associates 1988**

**Davis, Brody & Associates 1988**

# Kol Israel Synagogue

This synagogue is a combination of post-modernism and contextuality. The materials – red-brick, stone-banded walls and a red tile roof – echo the 1920s Mediterranean characteristics of the local architecture. As a solution to setback and height zoning restrictions, the entire site was excavated 10 feet 6 inches below grade. The main sanctuary was placed in this lowered space, rising up 34 feet. Three hundred and fifty seats were fitted into the surprisingly capacious interior. Oak balconies, timber ceiling beams and luxurious finishes including mosaic tile enhance this Orthodox Syrian temple.

ADDRESS 2504 Avenue K, Midwood
CLIENT Congregation Kol Israel
SUBWAY D to Avenue J
BUS B6, B9, B11, B44, B49
ACCESS none

Brooklyn

**Robert A M Stern 1989**

**Robert A M Stern 1989**

# Firehouse for Engine Company 233 and Ladder Company 176

An intellectual design, this is a process-driven project. Two grids, one based on the station's site and the other on the elevated mass-transit lines, overlap and intersect. The respective materials of these grids further differentiate and integrate the two frameworks. The ground level is placed within the existing grid of the site, reflecting its corner location by repeating the Cartesian street matrix. Square, coloured concrete block echoes the masonry of the neighbourhood. The upper level is skewed 45 degrees. Squares within squares (this was one of the first deconstructivist buildings), the two grids are joined at the front façade by a stainless-steel bay housing the central control rooms.

The exposed metal framework echoes the nearby elevated railway. Offices are located on the mezzanine level, which is apparent on the north elevation. Daytime and sleeping quarters are accounted for on different levels. A whimsical touch is the fire-engine red that appears intermittently as a straightforward reminder of the building's function.

Sculptural and evocative, this small but significant project, considered cutting edge when first erected, whets one's appetite for more. Most New York architecture is finance driven and therefore tends to be conservative and safe. Peter Eisenman is an international celebrity who has built all over the world. It is ironic that the only freestanding structure commissioned for his own hometown is this Brooklyn firehouse.

ADDRESS Rockaway Avenue and Chauncey Street, Ocean Hill
STRUCTURAL ENGINEER Robert Silman Associates
SUBWAY J to Clancey Street; L to Bushwick/Aberdeen
BUS B20, B25, Q24, Q56
ACCESS none

**Brooklyn**

**Eisenman/Robertson Architects 1985**

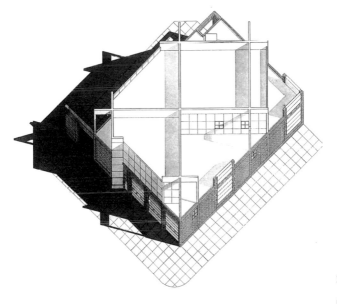

**Brooklyn**

**Eisenman/Robertson Architects 1985**

# Portable

# Carlos Mosely Music Pavilion

Dotted randomly across Manhattan are several highly visible tensile fabric structures. Patterns of perfection, they resemble bright white sea creatures in various states of repose. Complex geometries realised physically, they are like three-dimensional spatial studies from D'Arcy Thompson's tome *On Growth and Form*. Designed by the innovative architectural firm FTL, these structures are permanently temporary.

FTL is an acronym for Future Tents Limited. Preoccupied with the interaction between structure and form, its members were greatly influenced by the work of Frei Otto (with whom partner Nicholas Goldsmith worked in Germany for several years) and Buckminster Fuller. Engineering is integrated into their work along with the study of nature: minimal surfaces, soap bubbles, spiders' webs. The architects summarise: 'Form is about engineering and the materials used are directly related to form and engineering.'

One can sight these beautiful high-tech tents at the Port Authority Ferry Terminal, at the World Financial Center Winter Garden (see page 28), and at Bryant Park in the biannual Seventh on Sixth fashion extravaganzas.

The most mobile of these alternative urban forms is the nomadic Carlos Mosely Music Pavilion. Designed for the Metropolitan Opera and the New York Philharmonic, this tent is a portable orchestra shell. A polyester-membrane canopy stretched across three open-frame steel trusses, a foldable stage and 24 collapsible speakers can be assembled in six hours. The pavilion is transported by seven customised trucks, five of which are retrofitted to become part of the structure.

The stage is hinged, eight-panel marine plywood supported by lightweight aluminium beams. The edges and the rear centre rest on tractor trailer beds with undercarriages weighted with concrete ballasts. These

**FTL Architects 1991**

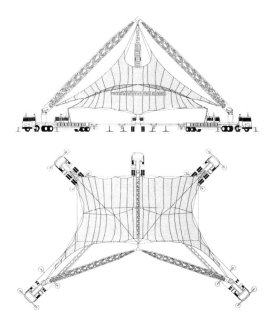

**FTL Architects 1991**

are necessary to counteract the thrust of the superstructure and tensioned membrane above. The membrane itself is 1/16-inch-thick polyester that has been sealed with PVC on both surfaces. It is dramatically hoisted into place with a winch and synthetic-fibre rope attached directly to the fabric.

ADDRESS temporary locations in 16 parks within all five boroughs of New York City
CLIENT New York Department of Cultural Affairs, New York Philharmonic & Metropolitan Opera
STRUCTURAL ENGINEER M G McClaren, Buro Happold
COST $3.4 million
SIZE 3120 square feet (290 square metres)
ACCESS open

Portable

**FTL Architects 1991**

Portable

**FTL Architects 1991**

# Index

New York: a guide to recent architecture

New York: a guide to recent architecture

New York: a guide to recent architecture

New York: a guide to recent architecture

New York: a guide to recent architecture

New York: a guide to recent architecture

New York: a guide to recent architecture

**New York: a guide to recent architecture**

ADDITIONAL PICTURES

page 51 Susanna Sirefman

page 165 reproduced by permission of Murphy/Jahn Architects

page 187 Jock Pottle, reproduced by permission of Kohn Pedersen Fox Associates

pages 195, 197 Christoph Kicherer

page 209 Kevin Roche John Dinkeloo and Associates

page 247 Kliment & Halsband Architects

page 253 Hardy Holzmann and Pfeiffer Associates

pages 261, 263, 265 Jonathan Moberly

page 269 Shigeo Anzai, reproduced by permission of the Isamu Noguchi Foundation, Inc.

page 287 The Brooklyn Academy of Music

page 303 Chris Lee1

**New York: a guide to recent architecture**